W9-CME-600

GROWING OLD
AND HOW TO COPE WITH IT

GROWING OLD
AND HOW TO COPE WITH IT

BY

ALFONS DEEKEN, S.J.

IGNATIUS PRESS   SAN FRANCISCO

255
CL
D

First U.S. edition published by Paulist Press
© 1972 by The Missionary Society
of St. Paul the Apostle

Cover by Victoria Hoke Lane

With ecclesiastical approval
© 1986 Ignatius Press, San Francisco
All rights reserved
ISBN 0-89870-104-x
Library of Congress catalogue number 86-80786
Printed in the United States of America

CONTENTS

I
On Growing Old

The Problem of Aging   9
The Process of Aging   14
Personal Individuality in the Aging
    Process

II   18
Coming to Grips with Old Age

Rejecting Old Age   21
Resenting and Envying the Young   22
Old Age "Drop-Outs"   24
Old Age Egoism   30

III
How to Grow Old Gracefully

Accepting Old Age   33
Learning Detachment and Wisdom   34
Facing the Problem of Loneliness   38
Repentance and Rebirth   46
Achieving Wholeness   53

Late Achievement   59
Fear and Anxiety   66
Overcoming Worries   72
Dealing with the Unexpected   74
Coping with Suffering   82
Finding Joy   88
Maturing in Faith   92
Finding Meaning   99
Marriage in Old Age: The New
   Encounter   108
New Religious Dimensions   115
Sharing in the Life and Love of the
   Trinity   128
"I Am Going to the Father"   140
Crossing the Desert into the
   Promised Land   145

Appendix
Man's Immortality and Eternal Life

The Problem of Immortality   149
Seven Approaches to the Question of
   Immortality   172
The Theological Approach to
   Immortality as a Confirmation of
   the Philosophical Hypothesis   175

What Is Eternal Life?   177
Marxist Critique of Heaven   185
Meaning of Belief in Immortality for
    Man's Life Today   187

I

ON GROWING OLD

The Problem of Aging

During several years of living in Japan, time and again I was impressed by one outstanding characteristic of the Japanese: their deep respect for tradition and for their elders. On entering a Japanese home one frequently sees a shrine in the family living room where reverence is paid to the ancestors. Although many behavior patterns are changing quickly, I am convinced that the deep bows of youngsters toward their parents and grandparents indicate that the Confucian sense for hierarchy has not been swept away by the process of Westernization. The prestige and the respected status of the elderly have a long tradition in Japan. As one of their neo-Confucian scholars put it, "Filial piety is what distinguishes men from birds and beasts."

In America, however, one does not encounter "Old is beautiful!" among the popular slogans of the day. Here, the problem
of growing old presents itself with greater
urgency than ever before in our history. As
statistics indicate, people today live longer
and, with a declining birth rate, the per-
centage of older people within the total
population is constantly rising. In 1850,
only 2.5 percent of America's population
was sixty-five or over. Today, 11.7 percent,
or 27.4 million Americans, belong to this
age bracket. It is estimated that by the year
2000 there will be at least 35 million Americans over the age of sixty-five.

Since so many in recent years have been
caught up with the problems of youth, the
problems of the increasing number of older
people have gone almost unnoticed. I refer,
of course, to a much wider range of problems than merely those of bed, board and
health. The welfare, social security and
Medicare programs are good, but they are
far from a panacea for the problems which
interest us most in this book.

Whereas the traditional Chinese and Japanese cultures have emphasized the relationship of the individual to the community, the civilizations of the West have, since the Renaissance, increasingly opted for the values of independence and autonomy of the individual. While glorifying these values, generation after generation in the West has largely neglected the equally important values of togetherness, solidarity and community. Conditions in America exemplify those of the West in general. Now we are begining to realize the one-sidedness of such an option. Young people have learned the lesson of independence extremely well, but the abyss between them and their elders gapes ever more widely. Today Western man is becoming keenly aware of the enormous price he has to pay for stressing individualism and independence: the price is isolation and loneliness. And it is the older people who have to carry the heaviest burden. Of them it has been said that they "are perhaps the loneliest generation that ever inhabited the face of the earth" (F. E. Crowe).

Simone de Beauvoir, in her monumental

study on old age, *The Coming of Age*, paints a gloomy picture of Western civilization's attitude toward its old. Old people, she claims, are often not treated as human beings. The young frequently mock, exploit and degrade them. In our Western society, age is a secret shame, or at least an embarrassment about which one does not speak. The purpose of de Beauvoir's book is precisely to break the conspiracy of silence, to shout from the rooftops that the way we treat our old people is criminal. In France, she tells us, elderly people are frequently placed in homes or hospitals by their children during vacation time, and after summer the children "forget" to bring them back. The prosperous nations of the West tend to treat their old people as a commodity that feeds the new booming industries of well-staffed retirement villages and nursing homes for those who can afford them; but the elderly poor languish under grossly inadequate care.

The Coming of Age, which became a worldwide best-seller, concludes with a call for radical reform. Since modern Western society treats its old so abominably, Simone de Beauvoir claims, there is need for a fundamental reform of society. The only way to remedy the nefarious situation will be to change the system. Our basic attitudes toward society, economy, value structure and toward life itself must change.

De Beauvoir has disturbed the tranquillity and complacency with which contemporary society treats old age. She has awakened the conscience of the West to rethink and reform its behavior toward the old. It would seem that basic structural reforms in our society are needed to bring about the conditions for a more humane life for the aged. It will take a great number of interdisciplinary studies to provide the scientific basis for these structural reforms.

But besides the question of social structures, of society's attitudes and of economic reforms, there is also the more important problem of the attitude the old people themselves must develop toward their old age, if indeed they want to master it. This book will concern itself with this particular task. There are few taboos left in our era of ever-increasing freedom and permissiveness, and yet, strangely enough, one's age remains for many people the last unmentionable, and it is a great insult to ask a woman over thirty how old she is. I will try to show that old age, far from being an embarrassment, is in fact a golden opportunity for human growth, fulfillment and deep happiness. The book will offer some practical aids, psychological and spiritual, that older people may find helpful to pass their years gracefully and use them fruitfully. Also, we hope that middle-aged people may find some of the aids useful to prepare themselves for the important period of later life. It is hoped that in the future more and more senior citizens will discover the unique opportunities that old age can offer them and that some will even begin to see for themselves that "Old is beautiful!"

The Process of Aging

Growing old presents one of the most difficult tasks in human development. Human nature seems to rebel against the dethronement of a man that takes place in the process of his getting old. Many people never come to grips with the great crisis of aging. For a while they fight against the inevitable fact that they grow old and gradually they arrive only at a state of embittered resignation. Then they give up all ambition, become tired and lose their vitality. For them, life at this point for all practical purposes comes to an end, even if they are still hanging on for a short while as aimless, grouchy citizens. One of the finest opportunities for growth and human development is thus wasted, because these people have not understood that the process of aging offers man a great challenge for maturing—for growing on the human level and for becoming more fully himself.

We are all familiar with the different age levels of childhood, adolescence and young adulthood. We also know how important and difficult it is to make the right transition from childhood to adolescence and then to young adulthood. The crises connected with these transformations are vividly before our eyes every day.

There is much less awareness that the transition from active middle age to old age brings a crisis of equal gravity. One does not hear much talk about it, because most people do not want to admit—either to themselves or to others—that they are growing old. We are living in a country that is characterized by a youth culture, so everybody feels he has to remain young or at least give the outward appearance of still being young. But this massive self-deception in our Western culture does not change the simple fact that everyone is, in fact, gradually growing older and has ultimately to face the crisis of old age. Our youth-oriented civilization only makes it more difficult for people to grow old gracefully, because the aging man and woman receive little understanding and support from society in this crisis of a personal transition to old age.

The reality cannot be escaped: every one of us, if not prevented by an untimely death, will come face-to-face with the crisis of old age. Every woman will sooner or later become aware that her bloom is fading. She will be conscious that her physical presence no longer holds the same attraction. People may still value her abilities, her professional success and her good reputation, but this will appear to her as little more than a retirement pension. Certain physical ailments will make themselves felt: slight disturbances of her powers of concentration, curtailed and lighter sleep, rheumatic pains and stinging headaches. The aging woman will be subject to moodiness, irritability and unrest. The vigor of life slowly decreases and weariness takes over. The mornings are losing the charm of newness, the noondays bring monotony, and the long evenings and nights are spent in loneliness.

When a man reaches the age of fifty or so he meets his noonday devil. Everything suddenly comes under question: his professional life, his relations to his fellow men, his sexual life. His family often has become smaller because his children have matured and left the family circle. Frequently he feels that his professional efficiency is decreasing, his creative power declining. Many a man, at this age, begins to lose his confidence and security. He is puzzled by what is happening to him. For a while he might have been proud of the new generation moving up, since he has produced it and can therefore enjoy its initial successes. But as the new generation gradually takes over, he begins to feel a twinge of distrust creeping into his previously benevolent attitude. These are the first external signs of the advancing crisis of aging. Interiorly, the chill is felt more deeply: "Life goes on! Is it possible that someday I will be no longer needed?" He who sits on the throne of life seeks to keep it; he will not easily give up or give in. And yet the thought comes creeping in that he could drop from life as a leaf drops from the tree.

Personal Individuality in the Aging Process

One of the more interesting discoveries of recent gerontology is that each person is in reality three different ages at once: the *chronological* age, which is determined by the number of years he has lived; the *biological* age, which is determined by the condition and state of his body; and finally, the *psychological* age, which is measured by how old a person feels and acts.

It is of great importance for an aging person to avoid a narrow, fatalistic view that makes the age marked by the calendar, the chronological age, the norm for one's feeling and acting. Some people age fast biologically precisely because they *feel* old. On the other hand, we have all met octogenarians who felt younger at heart than many people only half their age.

Most of us know of handicapped persons—these can be regarded, at least partially, as biologically old—who have performed feats which normally require the abilities of someone in complete physical health, that is, someone biologically young. John Milton, perhaps the greatest English poet next to Shakespeare, wrote a tremendous amount of sublime poetry during the last twenty years of his life—when he was completely blind! And Ludwig van Beethoven, widely regarded as the greatest composer of music in history, was even more incredible. He continued his composing until the end of his life, even though he was completely deaf for the last fifteen years! Think of the stupendous works of art (for example, Milton's *Paradise Lost* or Beethoven's Ninth Symphony) of which civilization would have been deprived if these two men had let their physical disabilities determine their psychological age.

II

COMING TO GRIPS
WITH OLD AGE

Rejecting Old Age

The description of the process of growing old which we have given shows that this stage of man's life is full of pitfalls. Here we will point out some possible dangers.

A great number of people simply reject the fact that they are growing old. They cling to youth as a caterpillar anxiously clings to a branch, refusing to become a butterfly that might swing itself into the new freedom of flight. Aging men and women often simply close their eyes to the evident facts and pretend that they are still young. It is sometimes pathetic to watch a middle-aged woman walking along Fifth Avenue trying self-consciously to appear much younger than she is. And the recent proliferation of cosmetics for men shows that they also are becoming less and less willing to look their age. Both sexes have failed to recognize that each age level possesses its own distinctive beauty.

Resenting and Envying the Young

A second pitfall at the time of aging is an attitude of envy and resentment toward the younger generation. Indeed, it takes a great deal of courage and magnanimity to see younger people enjoying the peak of their life without becoming somewhat envious and resentful. Only by a free and deeply interior letting go of what is proper to an earlier stage of life can one face this process of aging without fear and discontent.

If a man does not discover the new, important horizons that only older age can offer him, he will inevitably begrudge the young their seeming hold on life and develop a deep resentment against them. This danger of envy and resentment is particularly great in our Western civilization, which puts so much emphasis on youth and the advantages of youth. In pre-Communist China and in Japan, old age as such was highly honored and respected for its experience. For this reason, in both China and Japan, resentment had hardly any chance to develop. In our Western civilization today, however, there is little such respect for the experience of age.

Moreover, education and the modern mass media seem increasingly to fulfill the function that once was the prerogative of the old and experienced. Progress occurs so fast today that the old can no longer keep up with their juniors. The younger people have to learn and to be retrained so often that the old have not much to offer on the practical level.

Where the older generation *could* really offer valuable help, namely, in those areas requiring the wisdom that comes only from experience, they often do not feel sufficiently confident even for this task. Thus the generation gap grows wider and wider. The young do not feel that they need the old, and the old are fast losing their self-confidence. They live out their lives in bit-

ter resignation, envy and resentment. Sometimes they even take malignant joy over
certain evident failures of the younger generation. Even though it does no good, they
cannot repress the scornful "I told you so"
when some youthful project ends up on the
rocks.

Old Age "Drop-Outs"

In their declining years, most men and
women relish dreaming their lonely dreams of
a nostalgically remembered past. One of
the great temptations of old age is to escape
from an unfriendly present and an un-
promising future into the pleasant memories of the past. At the time of retirement it
comes as a great shock to many persons
that the attention and respect paid to them
by the community and family seem suddenly reduced. The result is often a loss of
self-esteem and a feeling of bitterness about
people's lack of recognition and gratitude.
Once the official position in the world of
profession and production is taken away

through retirement, former colleagues and subordinates often show considerably less respect for the old man. To the retired person, the world of the present appears suddenly very different, unfriendly, harsh, perhaps even hostile. His first reaction is to withdraw from it into himself and to become preoccupied with the past when everything was so much better. Returning to memories of their past, many aging people show a preference for their early life, the period of childhood and youth. Gradually, an idealized version of their past life emerges in the imagination and soon also in their conversation. "When I was young, we didn't behave like that. . . . People were really friendly then. . . ." As the community pays less attention to them and their self-esteem is slipping, many aging men are tempted to bolster up their own image of the past by exaggerating their accomplishments and glorifying their past greatness and importance. The works of literature are filled with such pathetic characters who try desperately to persuade themselves and whoever will listen to them that their past was more glorious than in reality it was.

To get down to some memorable examples, let us consider certain characters from a few of the best dramas of recent times. Doubtless many of us will recognize the shortcomings of these characters as more or less our own.

James Tyrone, the aging father in Eugene O'Neill's masterpiece *Long Day's Journey into Night*, and his dope-addicted wife, Mary, are examples of a couple nourishing an escapist attitude toward aging and a self-deceit about the past. In this autobiographical play, O'Neill portrays his actor father who used to play a single romantic role, that of the Count of Monte Cristo, for many years without further developing his acting potential. Compulsively stingy, he once entrusted his sick wife to a quack doctor who overdosed her with morphine. An addict ever since, Mary cannot face the crude reality of her declining years and attempts to escape into the unreal world of drugs. In a touching scene, she reminisces about her youth and, carrying her wedding gown in her arms, tries to recapture the past when she first fell in love with James Tyrone "and was so happy for a time". James, the aging actor, cannot face the truth about his own weakness, insecurity and miserliness. Haunted by a sense of inescapable doom, he attempts to forget the gloom of his declining years by seeking a refuge in alcohol. Both Tyrones have to wear masks, as it were, and create an unreal past that would appear less harsh than the unbearable anguish of the present. The painful catharsis demands from them that they tear away their masks and honestly confront their true personalities, flawed with all the mistakes of the past.

Another poignant example is Amanda Wingfield, the forty-five-year-old mother in Tennessee Williams' play *The Glass Menagerie*. She too is a person who lives in the past, in this case in the memories of social success when she was a Southern belle. Incapable of facing her present drab life in depression-time St. Louis, Amanda romanticizes the good old days when she grew up on a grand plantation in the South: she boasts that on one Sunday afternoon she received "seventeen gentlemen callers". Vulnerable and fragile like her crippled daughter's collection of glass animals—the "glass menagerie" of the title—Amanda is caught in the web of her memories, disappointments and fears. Her husband, a telephone man, deserted her when "he fell in love with long distance." The shy and crippled daughter Laura attempts to find refuge in the imaginary world of her glass animal collection. Amanda, the mother, lives in a world little more real than that of her daughter. In fact, her memories seem to have less reality than even the fragile glass, and Amanda, faintly realizing this, clutches after them all the more desperately.

The English playwright Terence Rattigan has created a literary figure in *Separate Tables* that personifies an attitude psychologists often find in residents of old folks' homes— the claim to a higher professional or social status than in reality they possessed. Major Pollock, the retired officer, who tries to appear self-assured and who loves to recount the military exploits of his past career, is gradually stripped of his glorious past. A pathetic old faker, he never reached the military rank he claims to hold; in fact, he was not even present in the battles he claims to have fought with such bravery.

We do not want to say that an aging person should banish all memories of youthful experience. One can profitably draw comfort and pleasure from such journeys into the past, and he should nourish a healthy pride in the accomplishments of his life's work. But he should beware of the great temptation to idealize and glorify his past life. Even more important, he must not give in to the temptation of escaping from the challenges of the present age by living almost completely in the past. These days there is much talk about young people who refuse to live with our present civilization, and are derogatively called "drop-outs". Must not old people who refuse to live in the present and escape into the land of memories equally be considered "drop-outs"?

Old Age Egoism

There is a fourth grave danger which an aging person must beware of: egoism. This often manifests itself in a kind of materialism. Tangible things become all-important; eating and drinking, the bank account, the comfortable easy chair. A senile caprice and selfishness show themselves in a lust for power, a desire to dominate, an attempt to tyrannize over one's own family and surroundings. Aging men and women feel that their strength is diminishing every day. The danger is that an overcompensation will set in through a domineering egotism, hardheartedness and limitless self-righteousness. In such instances a pathetic individual clings to everything he can still get his hands on, not realizing that life and all else are slowly but inevitably slipping away. Scrooge, the old miser in Charles Dickens' *A Christmas Carol*, is the classic literary portrayal of such old-age egoism.

When we speak of old-age egoists we are not referring only to those wholly unsympathetic individuals who on the verge of senility turn into parodies of their worst selves. Often a highly respected self-made man can become an unbearably self-righteous and willful egocentric in his old age. He is all the more tragic because he achieved so much in life, did so much good for others—and then in old age allows himself to slide into the role of a small family tyrant. He worked his way up from nothing, sacrificed every penny for his wife and children and now spends his final days lording capriciously over his family, telling them for the umpteenth time what a great guy he once was, how much he has done for them and how little gratitude he has received in return.

Robert Anderson has masterfully portrayed such a type in his movie and play *I Never Sang for My Father.* Tom Garrison, the octogenarian father of the play, has worked hard all his life, starting as a newspaper boy, working his way up to the top and retiring at a yearly salary of fifty thousand dollars. He has succeeded in life but in the process he allowed his ego to bloat to such proportions that it nearly sucks the life out of his forty-year-old son who is allowed to have only what his father sees fit to impose upon him. The old man never experiences temptations against faith in his unlimited self-righteousness. No real communication is possible with the father, for the old man knows he was successful in life. This fact seems, at least in his own estimation, to give him unlimited rights to judge, decide and control the life and destiny of his son.

HOW TO GROW OLD GRACEFULLY

Accepting Old Age

How can man face the crisis of aging in a positive way? Let's look at some positive approaches.

The first and most basic step is to accept the fact of one's growing older. It is wrong simply to endure the inevitable process of aging; one must positively accept it and say *yes* to this new stage of one's life. If a man or woman discovers the unique values and precious new opportunities that only mature age can give, then he or she will not just passively suffer the unavoidable but will actively and courageously walk through the gate that leads to the final stage of human completion and fulfillment. If you meet an older person you can usually find out very quickly whether or not he has come to grips with age. If he has, he will show composure and self-possession. If not, his interior disunity will reveal itself in unrest, complaints and absorption in trivial matters.

Learning Detachment and Wisdom

A second positive step in growing old peacefully is to learn an attitude of detachment. At the height of his life a person is usually so deeply involved in his daily business, his family and his property that he cannot look at the world with real detachment. He is too much a part of it all. With the process of aging, however, he can for the first time in his life acquire an attitude of profound detachment from the world. He can gain a certain distance from his surroundings and possessions and achieve a new perspective.

This new objectivity, this broad perspective or more total view, offers a deeper insight into the true meaning of everything: of life and love, of world and God, of time and eternity. A detached attitude allows man to see the true value of all things without the interference of egoistic personal interests or various kinds of biases and prejudices that used to dim his view of things in earlier years. If a man achieves this stage of detachment and objectivity, the younger generation will then approach him for advice, since they no longer will need to fear the force of his subjective selfish ambitions. The older person will have exchanged his throne of power for the seat of wisdom from which he can express himself in understanding and insightful advice for the younger generation. Having discovered his own new value, he can be appreciated by those who have less experience of life and are willing to listen to the voice of true wisdom.

Such wisdom of mature age is different from sharp intelligence or mere information storage. It cannot be learned from books, nor can it be acquired in schools and universities. Only by a lifelong process of gradual growth and maturing can this wisdom of the heart be acquired.

The world needs more than the youthful energies that press forward. It is also well served by the powers of wisdom that preserve the worthwhile elements of tradition. And who has more of these than the mature person who—we may as well admit it—is physically past his prime. The quiet goodness, wise patience and smiling calm of such mature persons can be an encouragement, a stimulant and a guide for others.

The liberating effect of detachment from self and the world and the new freedom of seeing all things in proper perspective through the eyes of faith are beautifully described in the great opening scene of Paul Claudel's play *The Satin Slipper.* As the play opens a Jesuit missionary is shown as the sole survivor on the wreck of a pirated, dismasted ship. Fastened to the stump of his main mast, he is drifting on the raging waters of the ocean, wholly at the mercy of the waves. Close to death, the Jesuit starts his last monologue:

> Lord, I thank you for bending me down like this. Sometimes, I found your com-

mandments painful and my will at a loss
and railing against your rule. But now I
could not be closer bound to you than I
am. However violently my limbs move,
they cannot get one inch away from you.
So I am really fastened to the cross, but the
cross on which I hang is not fastened to
anything else. It is floating on the sea.

This scene describes in a compelling
fashion the situation an aging man finds
himself in when he is approaching the end
of his life. With no solid ground under his
feet anymore, he is fastened to the cross,
and the cross is fastened to nothing, but
drifts over the void. The shipwrecked Jesuit
in Claudel's play knows that soon he will
sink, and yet, detached from land and life,
he discovers a new safety and serenity in
faith. A magnificient ease and self-forget-
fulness characterize the rest of the monologue. Sink he must, but he knows that it
will be a sinking into the arms of his heavenly Father. Thus, he can forget his own
fate and concern himself in his last prayer
with his straying brother, Rodrigo, the hero
of the play. Is not this the greatest triumph

of the Christian faith, that a man can, in the face of his own agony and death, still transcend himself and turn in loving concern to his fellow men?

Some Japanese martyrs, walking to their own crucifixion, so completely forgot their own impending death that they spent their last minutes trying to convey the glad tidings of their faith to onlookers on the roadside. They had learned this, of course, from their master who, even when hanging on the cross, did not complain about his own pain, but rather concerned himself with the well-being of others: entrusting his mother to the apostle John, consoling the good thief with the promise of paradise and even praying for his torturers who "do not know what they are doing".

Facing the Problem of Loneliness

For many people, coping with old age means coping with the problem of loneliness. For widows and widowers, the fearful and frightening awareness of being alone often becomes a depressing experience. Modern literature from Sartre to Williams is populated with aging characters haunted by the universal phantom of loneliness.

Numerous aging men and women confess that the suffering hardest to bear is this feeling of loneliness. Their old friends have died, one after the other. As one octogenarian put it: "There is nobody around anymore who calls me Jack." The children have moved away and want to lead their own lives. The intervals between their visits become longer and longer. And as man grows older he often finds it increasingly difficult to make new friends. The fear that he may appear to intrude on others prevents him from going out of his way to look for new acquaintances. If he is rejected even once, he easily becomes uncertain and doubtful about his own value and usefulness: Do people still want me, do they need me or do they just tolerate me? So he withdraws and spends many a night in bitter loneliness. What Tennessee Williams has one character say in *Orpheus Descending* will evoke an understanding response in this man: "We're all of us locked up tight inside our bodies. Sentenced you might say to solitary confinement inside our own skins."

Aging man should not too easily resign himself to loneliness. He should try rather to make himself available to others, keep up communication with his fellow men and possibly develop new relationships.

One concrete way would be to make regular visits to other old people who are living alone and will appreciate company. Getting involved in service to others is often the best way to overcome one's own loneliness and to take the mind off one's own suffering. For many oldsters membership in a Golden Age Club helps them to win new friends and to mitigate their loneliness.

If a person cannot move around anymore, letter writing might be a good opportunity to give a ray of hope and joy to other shut-ins and to prevent himself from getting isolated. Old friends and acquaintances may not be receiving as much mail as they used to and thus become more appreciative of little notes on birthdays, anniversaries and jubilees. Also, phoning older people who are living by themselves can be a fine way of cheering them up and of alleviating their loneliness and one's own.

An aging person who tries in these different ways to be of service to others and to show them some loving concern may have to spend many a day alone, but will never have to spend a lonely day.

But eventually the aging person might reach a point, especially in times of sickness, where communication is no longer possible, when he finally feels utterly isolated and alone. These are moments when there may be nobody to turn to but God. Then it is good to remember that our Lord understands what loneliness means, for nobody tasted the agony of loneliness more than Jesus Christ in the Garden of Gethsemani, and nobody tasted total isolation more than Jesus Christ on the cross.

The experience of aloneness need not be a negative experience. On the contrary, the emptiness of feeling alone can open man's heart and make him more perceptive of the presence of God, who likes to speak in silence. Loneliness can be a blessing. The experience of being alone can strip man of his masks and force him to confront his real self. It can deepen his faith and inspire him to seek a more personal relationship with God.

In the bitter hours of loneliness the only ray of hope and consolation might be the thought of God's presence. In spite of all appearances to the contrary, man is ultimately never alone since God is always there. Deepening one's awareness of God's presence can be an extremely rewarding way to fill the lonely hours of old age. Man either transcends his loneliness in a new personal encounter with God or he succumbs to its agony which in the extreme case can end in final despair. Our loneliness is often God's way of getting our undivided attention and of communicating with us on a new and deeper level.

In this connection I might briefly relate a rather personal experience which I myself had in a jungle in Vietnam. Working as a reporter, I got lost in a vast jungle and was walking for hours through the thick underbrush. Never before had I found myself so utterly cut off from all human beings. Suddenly, the quiet of the jungle was pierced by the rattle of a machine gun, I hurled myself to the ground. Were these South Vietnamese or Vietcong? Minutes earlier I had been searching desperately for human beings. But now, the physical closeness of humans whom I could not approach only heightened my feeling of being utterly alone. My face pressed to the mud, I waited and did not dare to move a limb.

In this hour of utter isolation and loneliness, suddenly some poetic verses came to my mind which I had often recited as a little boy without fully grasping the depth of their meaning:

> He who dwells in the shelter of the Most High
> and abides in the shade of the Almighty
> says to the Lord: "My refuge,
> my stronghold, my God in whom I trust!"

> It is he who will free you from the snare
> of the fowler who seeks to destroy you;
> he will cover you with his pinions
> and under his wings you will find refuge.

You will not fear the terror of the night
nor the arrow that flies by day,
nor the plague that prowls in the
darkness,
nor the scourge that lays waste at noon.

A thousand may fall at your side,
ten thousand fall at your right,
you, it will never approach;
his faithfulness is buckler and shield.

For you has he commanded his angels,
to keep you in all your ways.
They shall bear you upon their hands
lest you strike your foot against a stone.

On the lion and the viper you will tread
and trample the young lion and the
serpent.

The presence of God and his protective providence, so beautifully expressed in these verses of Psalm 90, suddenly became such a powerful reality that now, alone in a hostile jungle and surrounded by dangers, I felt closer to him than ever before.

If a man in his old age goes through the painful experience of loneliness he would do well to have always at hand some of the beautiful Scripture texts that assure God's children of his presence among them. Meditating on them we can deepen the awareness that ultimately we are never alone. Holy Scripture tells us again and again how close our God is. Saint Paul says to the Athenians: "God is not far from any of us, since it is in him that we live, and move, and exist" (Acts 17:28). When the Prophet Jeremiah shrinks back in fear from the mission that the Lord wants to entrust to him, God encourages and consoles him with the idea of his own presence: "Do not be afraid, for I am with you to protect you" (Jer 1:8). Joshua is reassured by the Lord: "Be fearless then, be confident, for go where you will, Yahweh your God is with you" (Jos 1:9).

The story of Christ's coming into this world tells of the new nearness of God: "They shall call him Emmanuel, a name which means 'God-is-with-us' " (Mt 1:23). One of the most moving words on the loving presence of God and his personal care for every human being, a word that has given new hope and courage to millions of

lonely people, is recorded in the book of
Isaiah: "Does a woman forget her baby at
the breast or fail to cherish the son of her
womb? Yet even if these forget, I will never
forget you" (Is 49:15). Again, the last words
of Christ to his apostles stress his con-
tinuing presence: "Know that I am with you
always; yes, to the end of time" (Mt 28:20).
With God being present nobody need ever
feel lonely again.

The great mystic Saint Catherine of Siena
said once that she could spend whole days
contemplating just one sentence from the
Creed: "His kingdom will have no end."
Each of us can find some prayer or verse of
Scripture which will help us over and over
again in times of desolation.

Repentance and Rebirth

When they reach their early fifties many
people become increasingly concerned
with a retrospective assessment of their
past. They are trying to take stock of their
past lives, of their glories and failures, their

accomplishments and omissions. In conversations some older men and women create the image of a life filled with successes and achievements. We are all familiar with the boastful monologues of aging people who relish reliving their past exploits by regaling their acquaintances with the rosy picture of an unblemished record of accomplishments. But when they are alone with themselves, when they cannot play this trick of wearing a mask to save face or bolster their egos and they look at their real selves from the vantage point of approaching eternity, most men and women of ripe old age become painfully aware of the abysmal gap between the ideals of their youth and their true achievements. If they are honest with themselves, they realize how often they wasted their energies, missed opportunities, pursued false goals and failed their community and family. Their whole past life appears to be a very unfinished and almost unrecognizable work of sculpture. They see some fine accomplishments, to be sure, but there is also a sense of disappointment and disillusionment induced by the awareness of many mistakes and omissions. And if a man can avoid deceiving himself he has to admit feelings of real guilt because he frequently acted selfishly, did not show enough love and compassion for his fellow men and often was not there when they needed him.

Unresolved guilt feelings about past wrongdoings or sinful omissions often create psychological disturbances in retired men and women. If the guilt of bygone days was not repented then, if no amends were made for unjust acts against one's fellow men, the painful memory of this frequently keeps an aging person awake and forces him to confront the ugly facts that he might have repressed for many years.

The retrospective assessment of one's past will always carry with it a grain of disillusionment, for who can say of himself that his life has been without sin? Everyone has to integrate his past into his present life and part of this task will often be an honest confrontation with one's suppressed guilt.

In a previous chapter we saw that it is childish and wrong for an older person to spend his last years reliving and recounting the glories of his past. But equally un-profitable would be the opposite extreme whereby a person spends his later years letting himself be haunted by the ghosts of fruitless remorse and be weighed down by the heavy burden of a guilty conscience. Psychologists and psychiatrists tell us that both extremes are, unfortunately, quite fre-quent among aging people and create a good proportion of health problems that could have been avoided if one had come to terms with this past in an honest and sin-cere way.

Max Scheler, in his brilliant essay "Re-pentance and Rebirth", presented us with a valuable approach to the problem of past guilt. Scheler starts with the question of whether something that was done in the past can be undone now, whether an evil deed can be blotted out again. It seems that the passing of time is an irreversible pro-cess and that what is past is simply past. This is true with regard to objective time within which physical events take place. But it is not so with *human time*. Man's existence is not like a river which flows by and cannot turn back and alter a part that has gone before and is past now. In contrast to the continuous flux of inanimate nature, which knows only one dimension and one direction, man still has power over the meaning and value of his past acts. He cannot alter the physical fact that a certain deed was done by him, nor can he change the external effects of his actions. But man can alter their internal meaning and value. Every event of our past remains somehow indeterminate in significance, incomplete in its value and still redeemable. In every moment of man's life the whole of his past is still present and in his power. In the act of repentance man has the capability of cancelling the quality of evil in past acts and of imprinting on them a new meaning and value. In repentance man reappraises part of his past life and shapes for it a new worth and significance. *Human time* differs from objective time precisely in this, that the former is not bound to the one-directional flux of inanimate nature. Man can still lay hold of the meaning and worth of his past deeds. Thus, repentance is an incursion into our own past life and an encroachment upon it. Repentance is the great power of self-regeneration and the most revolutionary force in the moral world. Since through repentance man really does have power over the meaning and value of his past acts, he can drive guilt out of the vital core of his personality, make his personality whole again and bring about his own moral, spiritual and religious rebirth. In popular opinion repentance has often been interpreted and then brushed aside as a mere impotent regret or a sorrowful looking back to past failures. For Scheler, repentance is more; it is a great paradox whereby man turns powerfully to the past to extinguish the quality of evil in past actions and at the same time works joyfully for the future, for liberation, renewal and rebirth.

These profound philosophical findings of Max Scheler have to be complemented with the theological teaching on repentance and rebirth in the sacrament of penance. The fact that there is a positive approach to the problem of past guilt makes it all the more tragic that so many old people suffer intolerably under the unrelieved burden of their own imperfect unredeemed past.

Christ is willing to say the words again that he addressed to the woman in the Gospel: "Your sins are forgiven" (Lk 7:48), whenever someone turns in repentance and love to him. And the words of Jesus which he spoke the night before his redeeming passion for the forgiveness of sins are also addressed to everyone today: "Your sorrow will turn to joy . . . and the joy no one shall take from you" (Jn 16:20–22). Some people seem to achieve a more intensive union with God in their old age because they are eager to make up for the failures of their past. The Church is aware of this aspect of sin and guilt, for she uses, in one of her most moving songs, the daring paradox of a "happy fault": "O truly necessary sin of Adam, which by the death of Christ was blotted out! O happy fault, which merited so great a Redeemer!" We all recognize these words from the Easter Vigil liturgy.

Achieving Wholeness

One of the encouraging and joyful experiences of many aging people is the growing awareness that their spirit can still triumph even when their physical powers abandon them. Psychologists and novelists alike have often described the process whereby an aging person is gradually deprived of his physical strength but is able to compensate for its loss by calling on inner reserves of strength from the depth of his spirit and soul.

We are all familiar with the general law of psychology according to which a physical handicap or the experience of inferiority in one field can act as a powerful stimulus to compensate in another field, in which a person may achieve extraordinary success. A young girl who is not blessed with physical beauty will often take it as a challenge and try to make up for her deficiency by excelling in learning or in sports. There she may well outdo all her more attractive classmates.

The same law of compensation applies to

old age. Experiencing the diminishments and deficiencies brought on by aging, an older person can take this as a challenge. The handicaps, trials and disillusionments of old age can then act as stimuli and incentives to arouse inner forces and creative powers that will help him to discover and develop new dimensions of his humanity and thus turn defeat into victory.

It is one of the saddest aspects of old age that many people seem not to be aware of their soul's power over the aging body and thus never develop the hidden potentials of their inner selves. It would seem that there are two possible paths of development in human life. In one case the mental curve follows the biological curve. This means that a person may still be alive in old age but his life is hardly human. With his mental activities and powers almost dormant, an aging person does hardly more than vegetate, without much joy and sense of human fulfillment. In the second case the psychological and spiritual faculties of the aging man remain functioning with great efficiency, and even significant original

thoughts or great works of art are not beyond his capabilities. The great German
writer Goethe expressed the deep insight
that in his younger years man lives *through*
his body whereas in old age he is forced to
live *against* his body.

There are potentials and forces concealed
in man that only start to evolve and unfold
at the time when the physical energies of
the body begin to diminish. During his earlier "working" life, a man usually concen-
trates so much on the energies which he
needs to earn his living that certain deeper
powers of his inner life remain under-
developed. Old age offers an opportunity
to discover and develop this deeper level of
himself. A systematic practice of meditation
and contemplation could be of great help to
unearth and unfold these treasures that are
waiting in the depth of man's selfhood.
Meditation and contemplation are not
quickly learned, but, once acquired, they
are tremendously rewarding.

In this connection I am reminded of several experiences where I administered the
sacrament of Holy Anointing to some older

person and afterward witnessed not only a remarkable restoration of spiritual strength but also a recovery of bodily health. The psychosomatic relationship is still a great mystery to us, but there definitely seems to be a close relationship between man's spiritual strength and his bodily health.

If success or failure in old age depends so much on whether or not one can remain intellectually alive despite the increasing deficiencies of one's body, then it should be of the utmost importance for man to prepare for his old age by developing his psychological, intellectual and spiritual powers to the highest extent possible. A gerontologist recently said that giving teenagers an intellectually more stimulating education and leading them to greater psychological maturity would be a greater contribution to the problem of old age than founding Golden Age Clubs. For many old people, the inner emptiness that suddenly opens up at the time of their retirement was there all the time; it was only covered over by their restless work. Developing interest and taste in intellectual pursuits, in art, music, literature and religion, is an important part of man's preparation for a fruitful old age. But even if a person has reached retirement age without the preparation for appreciating the fine arts, he should not give up easily in trying to appreciate them. A good instructor and great patience will bring surprising results.

On the strictly psychological level, the insights of C. G. Jung could be of great value here. According to Jung, man usually works and lives with only half of his psychic capability while the other half remains unused and forgotten. Former generations have been quite unaware of the astounding depths of the human being that have been uncovered during the past few decades. But even today most people seem to live with only a small part of their psyche while whole dimensions of their potential inner selves are neglected and ignored. Or, as Goldbrunner puts it, "many rooms of the house of the soul are closed and never opened."

The question arises, then: Is it justifiable for us to continue working with only half of our "talents" after we have discovered these immense latent resources of energy within all of us? Is there not a moral obligation to develop the unused energies of the soul and thus strive for the achievement of psychic wholeness? It has been said that although a man may do reasonably well during the first half of his life by using only part of his psychic energy, during the second half there arises a real need to make use of his vast latent potential; and the reason why so many people never reach human fulfillment or are consumed by boredom and inner void as they grow older is precisely because they have never discovered the potential energies that are stored in the depth of their soul.

According to Jung, making use of this newly discovered psychic sphere is essential both to achieving psychological health and to realizing a meaningful human existence. The integration of the conscious and subconscious parts of the soul and the achievement of an expanded psychic wholeness or completeness is, in Jung's view, not merely a psychological problem, but also a moral demand.

Once again, we want to stress that it is not too late to begin to develop the unexplored regions of one's personality even if a person has already retired. Patience and a positive, optimistic approach can work wonders!

Late Achievement

Earlier we saw that each person is in reality three different ages at once: the chronological age, the biological age and finally the psychological age. A man may be old according to the calendar and yet young in his psychological age.

If we look back into history we discover that, for many great men and women, chronological or biological old age was not an obstacle but frequently even an incentive to accept the challenge and achieve great things.

Even the ancient Greeks were aware of

the fact that although physical desires and abilities decrease with aging, a new horizon opens up in the realm of spiritual values. At the beginning of Plato's *Politeia* the aging Cephalus welcomes Socrates and tells him of his new interest in serious discussions on the basic problems of life. "For my part," he says, "as the satisfactions of the body decay, in the same measure my desire for the pleasures of good talk and my delight in them increase."

The mere fact that a person is old according to calendar age should not make him give up all plans for further achievements. The example of many famous men who achieved great things late in their lives could be a stimulus to exert the effort to remain young in one's psychological age.

Many outstanding literary, artistic and scientific achievements have come at an advanced age. The Greek dramatist Sophocles was eighty when he wrote *Oedipus Tyrannus*. Goethe was past eighty when he completed *Faust*. Daniel Defoe, after having tried out many different jobs, sat down to write *Robinson Crusoe* at the age of fifty-nine. In the following five years he produced six more novels. Immanuel Kant published his *Critique of Pure Reason* at the age of fifty-seven. Michelangelo was seventy years old when he completed the dome of St. Peter's. Verdi, Haydn and Handel composed immortal music after the age of seventy; Rembrandt and Monet painted some of their best pictures and Yeats wrote some of his greatest literature toward the end of their lives. Einstein and Schweitzer were creative even in their advanced years. François Mauriac, explaining the origin of his final novel, stated: "On my eightieth birthday, I said to myself, 'Since I seem to be a long way from dying, why not write another novel?' " He then wrote his last masterpiece, *Maltaverne*, which was published in 1969 when Mauriac was eighty-three years old. The novel became a best-seller in France.

In the field of politics, we can point to men like Churchill, Gandhi, Gladstone, de Gaulle, Adenauer and Reagan, who in spite of their old age made decisive contributions to the political shaping of their respective

countries. Gladstone became prime minis-
ter at the advanced age of eighty-four.
Konrad Adenauer was elected chancellor of
Germany in 1949 at the age of sixty-three.
At a time when people usually think of
retirement, Adenauer started a new, extraordinary career from which he would
emerge as one of the most successful political leaders in modern history. Reelected for
two more terms, he remained in office for
fourteen years, and retired from the chan-
celorship at the age of seventy-seven.

In numerous works of literature we find a
description of men and women who
achieved only modest goals or even failed
in their middle years, but reached true
greatness after a long struggle in their older
days. Sigrid Undset in her novel *Kristin Lav-
ransdatter* depicts the heroine Kristin in four
stages or dimensions of her life. First she is
a happy child, then a rebellious daughter;
next she becomes an estranged and bitter
wife. It is only toward the end of her life
that Kristin achieves, after great suffering,
genuine greatness and real heights of hero-
ism as a woman and as a Christian.

Some people develop, in the face of approaching old age, whole new dimensions of their humanity, resources that so far have been dormant and start blossoming during the very last years or months of their lives. Two fine examples of such late blossoming in the face of aging and death are portrayed in Morris West's novel *The Devil's Advocate* and in the magnificent Japanese film *Ikiru* (Living).

At the center of West's novel is an intellectual English prelate who has spent his life at a desk job for one of the Vatican congregations. Monsignor Blaise Meredith is a good man but hampered by a cold personality. In a sense, he is a one-dimensional man: disciplined, passionless, neat and correct. His personality lacks compassion and charity, a genuine understanding of the joys and sorrows, the passions and pains of people.

One day Monsignor Meredith finds out that he is under sentence of death. He is dying of cancer with only six to twelve months to live. The prelate is sent to an Italian village as a "devil's advocate" to investigate, for a possible canonization, the claim that Giacomo Nerone had really lived a life of heroic sanctity. From here on, the novel describes in a beautiful way the gradual transformation of a cold, dried-out, theorizing bureaucrat into a warm, understanding and loving priest. Meredith learns the deep truth that a man who does not love his fellow men cannot love God either. This man who has spent his life being precise, reserved and passionless, who admits that he has never hungered for anything, becomes now, during the last years of his life, personally involved in the glories and sufferings, the loves and frailties of the men and women of a tiny Italian village. At the end of the novel, it does not matter much whether or not Giacomo Nerone was really a saint and should be canonized. What is important is the glorious transformation of Blaise Meredith, who before his death from cancer has developed the richness of his own humanity of which previously he had never been fully aware. Meredith had left Rome as a desiccated pedant, with the dust of the libraries on his heart; he dies a compassionate, warm-hearted and human priest. *The Devil's Advocate* should become required reading for anybody who is approaching old age.

The film *Ikiru*, produced in 1952 by Japan's leading movie director, Kurosawa, has been called by several critics the greatest film ever made. It is a fascinating drama of an old man struggling to give meaning to his life when he finds out that he has cancer and only six months to live. Having spent all his years as a minor bureaucrat in city hall, the old man suddenly realizes that the achievements of his life do not amount to much. Now that his life's end is clearly in sight, he starts searching for the meaning of life. Already weakened by his illness, he desperately tries, during his last half-year, to do something for other people. With all his remaining strength he pushes a playground project through the multitude of obstacles of the local bureaucracy. The playground is built and the children of the neighborhood find a new paradise. During his last six months the stuffy old bureaucrat is gradually transformed into a compassionate human being who genuinely cares for others. In a final scene, a superb sequence, we see him sitting on the swing of the new playground, slowly moving back and forth, and humming a melancholy song. There he dies. *Ikiru* is a deeply moving film about the agony and the triumph of an aging and dying man whose last half-year becomes a powerful affirmation of life, love and meaning.

Fear and Anxiety

Fear and anxiety are threats and challenges awaiting most men and women when they enter old age. Fear of sickness and of death, fear about financial security and the gradual loss of friends, doubts about their sexual potency, fear of social isolation and loneliness—these are fears and anguishes that are lurking in the minds and hearts of many aging people. If some of the fears should prove to be justified, a frightening chain reaction may set in and turn the formerly self-confident oldster into a suspicious, anguished bundle of fears.

The theologian-philosopher Kierkegaard distinguishes between fear and anxiety. Fear refers to a definite and specific object which is the cause of fear, for example a snake or a disease. Anxiety, in contrast, is indefinite, unspecified, a mood that is not directed toward any particular object. Applying these two terms to the experience of old age, it would seem that for some older people it is the problem of anxiety even more than fear that is plaguing them. It is a general mood of anguish, doubt and uncertainty which has no clear and definite objects. Man feels himself threatened to the very core of his existence.

Fear and anxiety have a certain ambivalent character: they can be paralyzing and destructive, if man allows himself to be dominated by them. But they can also be salutary if man confronts them in the proper way and gains control over them.

The destructive force of fear and anxiety has been powerfully portrayed in the Japanese film *I Live in Fear.* An elderly president of a steel company in postwar Japan is suddenly gripped by the fear that his country will be wiped out by atom bombs. Gradually he becomes totally obsessed by this fear and tries to convince his family of the imminent disaster. He wants to sell the factory and move to South America but is stopped by his relatives. His family rejects the fear as unfounded and opposes the move as unrealistic. But the old man allows himself to be so dominated by his fears that finally, in order to force his family to flee with him abroad, he sets fire to his own factory and burns it to the ground. In a moving confession the old man admits his motives: "I am afraid, hopelessly afraid, and I am helpless before my fear. I can do nothing and my life has become a living hell."

Anxiety or dread can, however, also play a positive role in one's life. It can awaken a man from his lethargy and force him to confront his real self with its contingency and frailty, but also with its enormous possibilities. In his younger years, when man is more in control of his physical powers, he tends to rely perhaps too much on himself and is not sufficiently aware of his contingency and his ultimate dependency on God. The anxiety of old age can make a man newly aware of his true situation, namely, that in his own createdness and contingency he is really standing on the edge of a threatening abyss, preserved and supported only by the power of the continuous divine creation. Fear and anxiety can then be a healthy experience for a man, a challenge to confront the truth about himself. Kierkegaard goes so far as to scorn those who boast that they never experience anxiety because that means, he says, that they have not yet begun to exist as true human beings. For anxiety arises from the awareness of freedom and is thus a genuine expression of man as a person. The experience of anxiety could then be understood as anguish in the face of freedom. Kierkegaard sees in the experience of dread an eminently positive process which is necessary for man to transcend the limited concerns of everyday life and to reach out to the beyond. In this sense, he can say that learning to know dread is an adventure which every man has to confront if he is to escape perdition and that the man who has learned rightly to be in dread has learned the most important thing.

Quoting with approval a text of Hamann, Kierkegaard describes dread as an expression of some lack which prevents us from falling in love with the world. We feel a certain homesickness and uneasiness, and this becomes for us the fire and salt that preserve us from the decay of the passing age. Man can overcome dread in the face of fate only by entrusting himself to the loving providence of God, and he can overcome dread with respect to guilt solely by repose in atonement.

In modern literature, too, anxiety has often been depicted as a saving experience. What was a somewhat dry theoretical treatment in Kierkegaard found a lively dramatic description in the literary work of Gertrud von Le Fort and Georges Bernanos. Le Fort, in her novel *The Song at the Scaffold*, portrays a French girl at the time of the revolution. Blanche is full of fear, and when she enters a convent the nuns hesitate to accept her precisely because of her extraordinary anxiety. The strong self-confidence of the other nuns in the face of a threatening martyrdom at the hands of the revolutionaries appears in stark contrast to the uncertainty of the young novice. The experience of her own weakness and anguish leads Blanche gradually to a deeper humility and trust in God's providence. Out of weakness arise the power and strength of God's grace. And thus, in a typical Kierkegaardian way, dread becomes for her a saving experience by means of faith. When the other sixteen Carmelite nuns have finished their final path to the scaffold, Blanche suddenly frees herself from the shackles of fear and uncertainty and resolutely steps forth from the anonymous crowd of onlookers. She continues the *Veni Creator* that her sisters had only half finished when death silenced their lips and courageously faces her martyrdom at the hands of the hysterical women of the revolution. Bernanos wrote a film script version, *Dialogues des Carmélites,* based on Le Fort's novel. The key idea of Bernanos is well expressed in the felicitous title of the German play version, *Die begnadete Angst* (Graced Anguish). The words of the title may well be considered the briefest formula of a Christian interpretation of anxiety: anxiety is for the believer a blessed and salvific experience.

Overcoming Worries

Worrying seems to be a favorite pastime for many aging people. They worry about the past, they worry about the present, and, of course, they worry a lot about the future. Even many good Christians seem to be unaware that their faith could help to free them from numerous unnecessary worries that now make life harder than it needs to be. I once asked an elderly Japanese convert which aspect of Christianity had been particularly appealing to him on his way to the faith. Without hesitation this gentleman mentioned the passage of the Sermon on the

Mount, "Do not worry about your live-lihood, about what you are to eat, or what you are to drink, or how you are to clothe yourselves" (Mt 6:25–33). He said:

> I had spent an enormous amount of time during my life worrying about all sorts of things. I could never really feel relaxed and happy because I was always worrying about something. Worries about my work, worries about my health, worries about my children, worries about my future, worries about my growing old. Then I read this passage of the Sermon on the Mount on the providence of God who cares even for the birds in the sky and the lilies of the field. Suddenly I felt so peaceful and liberated from all my anxieties and fears, knowing that God cares for me too. I realized that with all my worries I had only made my life miserable.

Do we not all worry too much about too many things, and especially about the wrong things? Christ wants us to be joyful Christians, not gloomy ones who walk around full of problems and worries. And he also shows us how to free ourselves from torments and vexations. The liberating power is Jesus Christ himself. "Come to me, all you who labor and are overburdened, and I will give you rest. Shoulder my yoke and learn from me, for I am gentle and humble of heart, and you will find rest for your souls" (Mt 11:28–29). Saint Peter had deeply understood the idea of God's provident care and of the liberating power of Christ when he wrote: "Give all your cares to him, since he cares for you" (1 Pet 5:7). In faith, trust and hope and in our close personal union with Christ we can experience how he helps us carry our burdens and liberates us from our worries.

Dealing with the Unexpected

A frequent crisis for aging people is the sudden encounter with the unexpected. They are not ready to face it, and as a result they often turn bitter over some misfortune and sometimes never overcome their disappointment. For the rest of their lives they will keep telling everybody who is willing to lend an ear what a terrible injustice has been done to them. Sometimes the culprit they start blaming for their sickness or ill fortune is Almighty God himself.

Georges Bernanos in *The Diary of a Country Priest* has given us a classic portrayal of a woman who has become bitter against God because of a totally unexpected event, her son's death. In a poignant dialogue with her parish priest, the countess confesses boldly that she has never forgiven God for taking her son. In her bitterness she hates him whom she holds responsible for her son's loss. Her heart poisoned with resentment, she alienates her own daughter and drives her to the edge of suicide. The priest, sympathizing with the agony of this tortured woman, quietly tells her that she can shake her fist at God, spit in his face, scourge him and finally crucify him, but it would not really matter, since it has already been done to him. On the verge of death, the countess finally realizes that "Hell is not to love anymore." She had isolated herself from God in bitterness and hatred and thus created her own hell on earth. But even for her, the ultimate answer lies in the unforgettable words which conclude *The Diary of a Country Priest:* "All is grace!" Divine grace finally breaks through the hard shell of her embittered heart and rekindles the embers of love.

In hospitals one often hears old people ask: What did I do to deserve this? These people seem to believe that God is punishing them for some past sins. But from God's self-revelation in the New Testament we know with certainty that our God is not a vindictive God. Christ suffered more than any other man, and he certainly did not "deserve" it. What woman went through more hardships than our Lady, and she did not do anything to "deserve" it. The greatest pains on this earth were suffered willingly out of love.

I have listened to so many old people telling me their "story" of how God or their fellow men have failed them that I wonder whether these men and women do not approach their old age with basic misconceptions and wrong attitudes. Their image of God is all too human. They seem to believe that their faith was meant to work somewhat like a social security pension: I go regularly to Mass on Sundays, turn in my collection envelopes, say my daily prayers and as a return for that God has to do his part and take care that everything will go well and that my declining years will be entirely halcyon and smooth-flowing.

The simple fact is, of course, that life does not turn out that way. Those who have tried hard to serve God during the previous parts of their lives seem to be particularly prone to run into unexpected problems in their later years, as the story of Job indicates. The right attitude and the proper preparation—as far as we can ever be sufficiently prepared—is a strong faith that God is the absolute Lord and that he really knows better than we do what is best for us.

I once experienced a moving example of such a genuine Christian faith in the absolute lordship of God and of trust in the mysterious ways of God's providence. During my stay in South Vietnam, I visited the Catholic refugee camp of Honai near Bien

Hoa. In a sense I was lucky that I got to Honai at all, since just after I had left Bien Hoa the Vietcong exploded a bomb at the place where I was staying. In the refugee camp were about thirty thousand Catholics who had fled Communist-ruled North Vietnam after the Geneva Agreement split their country in two. At that time, approximately 1.2 million North Vietnamese had fled to the south, about eight hundred thousand of them Catholics.

Most of the refugees at Honai had been well-to-do farmers. But when they realized that their part of the country had turned Communist and that consequently they would not be allowed to practice their faith freely or to give religious education to their children, they undertook the enormous sacrifice of leaving their farms and gardens, their houses and all their property. As penniless refugees they fled to the south and had to start again from scratch. The South Vietnamese government settled them in the midst of a large forest, where they had to start cutting the trees to build their small huts. When I walked through the Honai camp I saw the many small wooden huts in which they had settled, but to my amazement I also counted twenty-four chapels, and these were the finest buildings of all. Even on weekdays, these chapels were packed by those hard-working refugees, and for me it was a most moving religious experience to hear their voices as they prayed and sang—voices that could not hide the hardships and sufferings they had gone through, and yet at the same time voices that expressed deep, mature faith, hope and Christian joy.

Talking to an elderly carpenter in this refugee camp, I found out how unpredictable and difficult his life had turned out to be. Originally he had lost the house he had built in North Vietnam. Fleeing from the Communist part of his country, he built a new home in a village north of Saigon. One day the Vietcong came and burned his place down. He told me that only recently he had arrived in Honai and now was starting again from scratch. To me, this Vietnamese carpenter seemed like Job in the Old Testament. Because of these experiences I thought I would find him bitter. And who would have been able to blame him for that, after all he had gone through? I could recognize the marks of suffering and pain on his wrinkled face. Here was a man for whom deprivation, disillusionment and affliction had become a way of life. There was no external comfort to fall back on, no tangible, visible success to be proud of—for most of the houses he had built had been burned down or might be destroyed any day. There were only his two hands left to work with and—what made all the difference in the world—his profound confidence and trust in God. For he was a man of deep faith. Listening to his life story, I heard not one word of complaint. This man was even grateful to God for the way he had guided his life, and the spirit of Christian joy had finally triumphed over disillusionment and depression.

Ever since my encounter with this Vietnamese carpenter, he has become for me the prototype of what a genuine Christian should be: a man who believes that God is a loving and provident Father, but also the absolute Lord of his life. He is a man who believes that a Christian has to remain open to the unexpected in life, ready to do the will of God even when it means, humanly speaking, catastrophe and always starting anew.

When I drove back on the dusty road from Honai to Saigon, I reflected on the courage and faith of the North Vietnamese Catholic refugees, and I could not help thinking of another event that took place many centuries before: God's call of Abraham away from his native country into a yet uncertain future. Abraham was already a "senior citizen" at the time of the call. "The Lord said to Abraham, 'Leave your country, your family and your father's house for the land I will show you.' . . . So Abraham went as the Lord told him. . . . Abraham was seventy-five years old when he left Haran. And he set off for the land of Canaan . . ." (Gen 12:1–5). In Abraham's life, too, God was the absolute Lord whose will was decisive whenever the patriarch faced a major decision. And God demanded great things of Abraham, as he did of the Catho-

lics in Vietnam. Both Abraham and my carpenter friend in Honai were, in their old
age, led on an unexpected and difficult
road toward the maturity and completion of
faith.

Perhaps many old people would say that
they have never really felt that God was at
all close to them, much less that God ever
seemed to be speaking to them as he did to
Abraham. But Abraham was already a very
old man before he was called by God to do
his essential work. If the aged have the
patience to develop a life of faith and openness to God, they will recognize his call in
many instances or situations where they
formerly were deaf to that call. And sometimes God will be asking very difficult
things of them. Will they have the faith and
courage of Abraham?

Coping with Suffering

Old age offers man a unique opportunity to
share more deeply in the passion and res-

urrection of Christ. The aging person realizes in a more intensive way what every
Christian in some sense is called to do during his whole life: to participate in Christ's
Passion and his redemptive suffering and
to bear witness to and share in Christ's
Resurrection and glory. In the afflictions of
old age man experiences in a new way the
meaning of Christ's words, "Unless a grain
of wheat falls into the earth and dies, it
remains alone; but if it dies, it bears much
fruit" (Jn 12:24). For a person of faith the
anguish and agony of old-age sufferings
are as painful and as real as for anyone else.
But he knows that Christ never promised a
paradise on earth. On the contrary, he
warned Saint Peter about what would hap-
pen in his old age: "I tell you solemnly,
when you were young you put on your belt
and walked where you liked; but when you
grow old you will stretch out your hands
and somebody else will put a belt around
you and take you where you do not wish
to go" (Jn 21:18). Many aging men and
women experience painfully in their old age

that they cannot walk where they would like to and have to go where they "do not wish to go".

At times, aging men and women experience the anguish and agony of total desolation, and even the thought of God's providence does not offer them any emotional consolation because God seems to remain silent. Shusaku Endo, the leading Catholic novelist of Japan, has described such extreme agony of man in his novel *Silence*. The title refers to the silence of God in the face of uttermost human suffering. Endo depicts the anguish of the Catholic Japanese who in the great persecution of the early seventeenth century were hung head down from a gallows and let down into a pit filled with stinking excrement. Some martyrs lived through such agony for several days and nights. It was a heroic test of faith, but even in the face of God's apparent "silence" many martyrs clung in faith to God even unto death.

For many aging people there comes a time when loneliness or physical suffering seems truly unbearable. Working as a chaplain in a New York hospital, I often met such patients, and it was moving to see the heroic courage with which they bore the seemingly unbearable. One important motive and source of strength for such persons is the belief that suffering, if willingly accepted and endured in union with the suffering of Christ, can have redeeming power for the salvation of other men. This Pauline idea can be a tremendous help for an aging and suffering man. Turning one's attention to a loving concern for others is perhaps the best way to transcend one's own misery.

I will never forget one evening in a New York hospital, when an elderly lady suffering from cancer explained to me what the following two passages from Saint Paul meant to her: "If we are afflicted it is for your salvation" (2 Cor 1:6) and "Now I rejoice in my sufferings for your sake" (Col 1:24). "These two Scripture texts", she said, "give a profound meaning to my sickness. I can offer my sufferings for other people and in this way help them to achieve salvation. Confined to this hospital bed, I still can help other people to come to the faith and to enjoy the hope and joy that Jesus Christ bestows on those who believe in him. At the same time, this slow dying to which my sickness has condemned me has become easier for me since I began to see a meaning in suffering."

The experience of suffering in old age takes on its deepest meaning when it is seen and accepted as a sharing in the agony of Christ in Gethsemani and on the Cross. The whole life of a Christian is a walking in the footsteps of the Master, but it would seem that for many Christians it is only in old age that they are admitted to share fully in the agony of Christ's last days on earth.

Christ tasted the bitterness of loneliness and the anguish of impending pain in the garden of Gethsemani to such an extent that he cried out: "My Father, if it is possible, let this cup pass me by" (Mt 26:39). Saint Luke, with the eye of a medical man, adds an observation that reveals the whole depth of Christ's affliction: "In his anguish he prayed even more earnestly, and his sweat fell to the ground like great drops of blood" (Lk 22:44). And then the painful words on the Cross: "My God, my God, why have you forsaken me?" (Mt 27:46). In the anguish of his Passion and death, Christ experiences the contingency and frailty of human nature in the most extreme form. But through it all shines forth also the splendor and the majesty of God: "Nevertheless, let it be as you, not I, would have it" (Mt 26:39) and "Father, into your hands I commit my spirit" (Lk 23:46).

In the experience of suffering, aging man is offered a glorious opportunity to gain a deeper understanding of Christ's anguish and passion, to participate in the fate of his last days on earth and to have a foretaste of the Resurrection and the new life to come.

The Christian, real as the agony of his old age may be, knows of the close link between the suffering and the glory, the Passion and the Resurrection. Saint Peter put it this way: "Now I have something to tell you elders: I am an elder myself, and a witness to the sufferings of Christ, and with you I have a share in the glory that is to be revealed" (1 Pet 5:1). Ultimately, the aging Christian knows that his old age is not an end but a beginning, and that beyond the doom of death is the dawn of never-ending life.

Finding Joy

Some forms and expressions of joy and happiness that were characteristic of earlier stages in man's life no longer possess the same attractiveness in old age; others are not accessible anymore. For example, participation in physically demanding sports, traveling and the fascinations of youthful love may have been sources of happiness and joy in earlier years; for most oldsters they are only memories. It would be unfortunate for an aging person to daydream excessively about forms of joy that are now beyond his reach. In the course of life, one must gradually develop a sense for new types of joyful experiences. Man is created to be joyful, and he has to experience joy if he wants to be fully human. Many aging people make their lives unnecessarily hard because they are blind to the good things that God offers them at this stage of life, experiences, that should be enjoyed.

Each person has to discover in his own way the joys of old age. For some it may be the grandchildren who become a source of delight and satisfaction. Others may develop a new interest in the enjoyment of art, music and literature, or they may experience a new pleasure in the splendor and beauty of God's creation. A healthy pride in the achievements of one's life will offer a feeling of satisfaction to many retired men and women. A growing number of older people are finding great profit in Bible classes offered by the adult education programs of numerous parishes. Reading regularly the Sacred Scriptures, many aging persons discover the "glad tidings" on a new level of depth and understanding that they have never known before. In fact, the very name "Gospel" means "good news". Therefore, anyone who reads the Gospels without joy is not reading them in the same spirit in which they were written.

An aging person should make a positive effort to develop a sense of joy in making himself unobtrusively available for others. He will be surprised how much joy there can be in the simple efforts of being kind to others and of being available for those who need him. Because an aging person develops a more nuanced sensitivity and appreciation for kindness shown to him, he is also able to be more sensitive toward the needs of others and can find new delights in showing them personal attention and love.

God wants us to be joyful Christians. This is one of the principal impressions that a frequent reading of the New Testament will give us. God is doing everything in his power to imbue us with his deep unending joy. Christ points repeatedly to the providence of his heavenly Father to banish all anxiety and fear from his followers. He encourages us not to worry too much and especially not about the wrong things. Even on the night of his own passion and in the face of his impending death, Christ emphasized again that the life of a Christian should be a joyful one: "These things I have spoken to you, that my joy may be in you and that your joy may be full" (Jn 15:11). Saint Paul, a genuine interpreter of the Master, keeps repeating that the Christian faith is a joyful message of glad tidings. Joy is for Saint Paul the sign that a man has true faith; joy is the fruit of the Holy Spirit. "Rejoice in the Lord always; again I say, rejoice" (Phil 4:4). Some might suspect that Paul, who writes so much about joy and rejoicing, must have been safe and secure, somewhat remote from the anguish and the pain of everyday human life. But Paul was no stranger to human suffering. He knew the grim realities of a life hounded by per-secution. The words about rejoicing in the Lord were not written under a green tree on a bright Roman spring morning or on the writing table of a comfortable home, but in a grim prison cell where Paul was awaiting trial (Phil 1:12–16). Paul has deeply understood the central message of Christ and thus he can write about the beautiful

Christian paradox, that in faith his heart is
filled with joy even in the midst of loneliness, anguish and pain.

Maturing in Faith

As a man grows old, many things that he
previously took for granted are called into
question. His job, his health, his sexual
power, his economic security—all these
suddenly look much less stable than they
appeared in bygone years. It should, then,
not come as a great surprise that new
doubts also creep into a man's religious
faith. After all, faith was, to a greater or
lesser extent, part of the whole web of life,
and at this stage of aging it is the total life of
a man that is subjected to a new question
mark. The problem is very grave if a man's
faith has not sufficiently developed and
matured during his adult life. In this case
the total questioning of life in old age will
hit all the harder.

An aging man has to make a total transition to a new stage of life, and since faith is

an essential part of his life, faith also has to be deepened and matured on this new level of life.

Some people who have always lived according to the Christian faith are terror-stricken when, in their old age, they are suddenly confronted with a profound crisis of faith. They sometimes do not recognize this experience for what it is, a final God-given opportunity to grow through darkness and doubts to a more mature and loving faith. Faith does not always give the inner experience of consolation and joy, but often it leads man through the valley of darkness and mist.

During my student years I had a personal experience in which I came to see a symbolic expression of our life of faith.

I was one of a group of students studying in Munich and spending our summer vacation in the Swiss and Austrian Alps. One day we decided to climb Mt. Schesaplana in Austria, a mountain about eight thousand feet high. Around five o'clock in the morning we started climbing. As we climbed higher and higher we entered into a dark sea of mist. The mist became so thick that we could not even see the path thirty feet ahead of us. Of course, we had no vision of the summit. Every time we sat down for a few minutes, fewer words were spoken, but we could read in each other's eyes the growing doubts: Was it feasible at all to continue? Would we ever reach the summit? And would it be worthwhile even to reach the top of Mt. Schesaplana if it was covered with mist? The only guarantee we had was the word of a friend who, down in the valley, had explained to us the route by which we would reach the summit of Mt. Schesaplana and discover a majestic Alpine view.

Although discouraged and exhausted, we decided to go on climbing. And then the unexpected happened. Suddenly, we broke through the wall of thick mist and found ourselves above the floating clouds. Looking upward, the dazzling sun shone forth so radiantly that it blinded our eyes. Before us, within short reach, lay the summit of the mountain. All around us were the majestic snow-covered mountaintops of the Alps. We could look far into Italy, Switzerland and Germany—a majestic sight of overwhelming beauty, far surpassing anything we had ever seen before. And below us, like a big sea, were the misty clouds covering and darkening the Alpine valleys.

When afterward I thought of this grand experience in the Alps, I came to see in it a striking symbol of our life of faith. In our life of faith, too, we have to walk for many hours through mist, neither seeing the goal we are walking toward nor having any guarantee of its reality except the infallible word of Jesus Christ in whom we believe.

Doubts arise in our hearts; the path is steep at times; we get tired and exhausted. Frequently we look back into the valley of a purely natural existence and are tempted to give up and return there. Should we not be satisfied with living in the valley? Since we know so little of what is awaiting us at the summit of our life of faith, is all the effort really worthwhile? Emphatically *yes*, since in the midst of all these doubts there is a voice within us urging us to go on climbing, a voice that tells us of that majestic beauty that lies beyond, a beauty which will surpass our highest expectations. As Saint Paul says, there await us "the things that no eye has seen and no ear has heard, things beyond the mind of man, all that God has prepared for those who love him" (1 Cor 2:9).

The experience of darkness and dryness, of desolation and misty hours, can have a deep significance in our life of faith. To walk at times through hours of darkness can help us to grow in faith. If we always experienced a deep consolation in prayer, at Mass and in our whole spiritual life, it would be easy to be religious. But God also wants to give us an opportunity to prove our love for him in hours of desolation and loneliness. And thus he lets us walk through the gray shadows of mist and clouds by the light of faith alone. Saint Paul emphasizes the difference between the present life and the future: "Now we are seeing a dim reflection in a mirror; but then we shall be seeing face to face" (1 Cor 13:12).

Our relationship to God is in many ways

similar to our relationship with other human beings. If someone loves us and showers us with constant attention, it is not hard to respond to this love. It does not cost us a great effort, nor does it prove that our love has any real depth. But once a crisis arises, and we do not feel anymore the warmth and attention of a loved and loving person, when misunderstandings arise and all the joy and consolation of the first love have gone, then we have the opportunity to prove that our love has depth.

Our faith in God goes, during the different stages of our life, through a similar development of growth and maturing. A crisis of faith can become very significant for us. It challenges us to make a new personal decision, to make our religion a more personal possession and our faith a more personal commitment.

Sometimes a crisis of faith simply means that we have remained too long in a previous stage of development in our life. At every stage of our lives we have to make a new commitment to Jesus Christ, or, better, we have to renew our basic commitment to him in the light of each of our new significant experiences.

Josef Goldbrunner, a famous Munich catechist and psychologist, offered a felicitous comparison of man's conversion process which we can also apply to man's gradual growth in faith: "This lifelong process of conversion acts like the constantly repeated passing of a magnet over iron, so that in time all the molecules group themselves in one direction." Applying this image, one could say that, in the lifelong process of renewed faith commitments, man groups all the molecules of his being in faith, hope and love toward the triune God and in loving concern toward his fellow men.

Old age would seem to possess a specific significance for the growth and development of our faith. This final crisis of faith can challenge a man to reach out and make a final effort to achieve full maturity of faith and love. I have met some fine Catholics who went through terrible struggles to retain their faith during the very last weeks of their lives. Even a great saint like Thérèse of

Lisieux suffered a real agony of doubts and uncertainties, of darkness and interior emptiness on her very deathbed. Her sisters were horrified to hear from such a saintly person the admission that she was "assailed by the worst temptation of atheism". It seems that God frequently offers a person in the very last days of his life an opportunity to grow to heroic faith and love.

Finding Meaning

One of the key problems of aging people is the frightening thought that there might not be much meaning to life in their old age. Gradually it dawns on them that, perhaps, one day they might not be needed anymore at their place of work, in their family and in society. When man becomes aware of the gradual decrease in his physical and mental powers, he begins to fear that he may become useless and unwanted, a burden to others. Especially people who have led a very active life, who have striven for great achievements and whose minds have been absorbed by the pursuit of great projects in life, will feel a real terror at the sudden lack of purpose and meaning in their lives at the time of their retirement. Many people at this stage develop neuroses and various psychological imbalances due to the seeming emptiness and aimlessness of old age.

One of the most horrifying developments of our times is the great jump in the rate of suicides. Thoughts of suicide come to a person precisely when he sees nothing to live for. That there is much frustration and despair among older people is evident from some statistics. In France, the suicide rate for the general population is 19.6 per 100,000 people; but for the age group over 55, taken separately, it climbs to 158.0. A recent statistic in Germany showed that whereas 21 out of 100,000 Germans commit suicide annually, among the 60-year-old men the suicide rate is 55, and the number of women aged 50 to 55 who take their own lives is double that of the age group 30 to 35. And, as one commentator dryly remarked, the suicide attempts of older people are nearly always successful. England and the United States display the same characteristics: the suicide rates increase gradually with age. In England, three times more men in the age group 40–59 take their lives than men under 40, and among men over 60 the suicide rate is even five times higher. In the United States, the suicide rate for males of the age group 45–54 is 22.5 per 100,000; for the age group 75–84 it climbs to 41.4; it reaches its peak in the age group 85 and over where 50.2 per 100,000 take their own lives.

How important it is to discover and develop a new sense of meaning for the later part of one's life has been newly emphasized by the so-called Third Viennese School of Psychotherapy, in the logotherapy of Dr. Viktor Frankl. Although Frankl's insights on the psychological importance of meaning in life are aimed at all age groups, they seem to have particular relevance for the period of transition to old age.

Frankl rejects both Freud's idea that

human beings are driven mainly by sexual energy, and Adler's claim that power drives are the fundamental human strivings. Rather, Frankl insists, it is the search for meaning in life that must be considered as man's main concern and most basic striving. Logotherapy—"logos" for Frankl signifies "meaning"—focuses on the meaning of human existence, trying to assist the patient to find meaning in his life. Frankl, who himself lived through the hell of Auschwitz, is fond of quoting Nietzsche's words:

"He who has a why to live for can bear with almost any how."

If a man has a *why* to live for, he has achieved an outlook on life that cannot help but have a beneficial influence on his psychological health. On the other hand, if a man fails to see any meaning in life and experiences frustrations, inner emptiness and an "existential vacuum", his mental health is gravely endangered; such a psychological state frequently results in neuroses, a major health threat to twentieth-century man.

The immensity of this problem can be seen in the many manifestations of existential vacuum in our days: boredom, "Sunday neurosis", alcoholism, juvenile delinquency, the inner crisis of pensioners and aging people. The frustrated desire for meaning is frequently compensated for by an exaggerated desire for power, expressed in the desire for money, or by an extreme drive for sexual pleasure. Underlying all these destructive phenomena is a failure of the sufferer to find meaning in his existence.

To the question "What precisely is the meaning of life?" each man must find his own answer. A logotherapist refrains from imposing value judgments on the patient, leaving it to the patient to find the meaning of his individual life. Frankl stresses, however, that the meaning of our existence, while unique for each individual, is not invented by ourselves, but discovered. The logotherapist's role is to broaden the patient's field of vision and to help him become aware of the whole wide spectrum of meaning and values. No value judgments are imposed on the patient; rather, truth itself and the richness of meaningful reality are made visible to him in a new light.

Although logotherapy would not limit the search for meaning to a religious interpretation of life, it does, in contrast to Freud, take a sympathetic view toward faith, and considers religious belief an eminently valuable meaning orientation for man.

Many old people express their feelings of lack of purpose and meaning in phrases like "I am no good for anything anymore" or "I am useless and not needed anymore." Nurturing such feelings of frustration will have a detrimental effect on a man's self-esteem and will often create a serious inferiority complex. Old people have a psychic need to feel that they are still useful and still needed. The younger generation and society at large should recognize this need and respond to it by allowing and encouraging them to contribute their wisdom, experience and skill for the benefit of family and society.

The concrete search for meaning and

purpose in old age can take many different forms, depending on a person's health, skills and the concrete situation of his life. For some oldsters, assuming household responsibilities for their married children and baby-sitting for their grandchildren can banish the fear of void and return a new sense of purpose and joy to their old age. Many older men feel suddenly younger again when they are asked to give advice; the feeling of being useful and needed boosts their diminished self-esteem and gives new meaning and purpose to their lives.

Living in a mass society, many people today, especially older ones, underestimate their own importance. They feel that whatever they do cannot make a great difference anyhow, and thus they "bury their talents". We Christians, and elderly Christians in particular, need to be reminded that if we really live a genuine Christian life, we can make a great difference, we can make this world a better place to live in and we can help others to become more fully and more

joyfully human. True and complete humanity goes hand-in-hand with mature Christianity.

To show how much one Christian can do
to bring Christ into this world and to
change the hearts of men, let me briefly
recount the life of a great Japanese woman
whose enormous influence I myself witnessed in Tokyo. Her name was Satoko
Kitahara. The daughter of a university pro-
fessor, she lived in a rather well-to-do sec-
tion of Tokyo. While still a student at a
Tokyo university she discovered Christ.
She was baptized in 1949 at the age of
twenty-four. Through various circumstances
she got to know the ragpickers in the slums
of Tokyo. Their hard life convinced her that
Christ was calling her to meet him in the
person of these ragpickers. She gave up the
easy life of her rich family and moved into a
slum area to be near the suffering and
needy. With her, new joy and hope entered
the ragpickers' colony; the underprivileged
children especially found a personal friend
in Miss Kitahara. Once, when one of the

ragpickers got sick and consequently the whole family began to starve, Miss Kitahara herself took the old ragpicker's cart, pulled it through the streets collecting rags and thus supported the sick man's family. Eventually, the hard work proved to be too much for her frail body. She contracted tuberculosis and died in 1958 at the age of thirty-three.

Miss Kitahara's fine Christian charity caught the imagination of the Japanese people. They were so impressed that this girl had sacrificed herself for the well-being of the ragpicker colony that a short while later a splendid film was made about her life. On the anniversary of her death Japanese television offers lengthy programs about her, and her biography became a popular book in Japan. Millions of people experienced for the first time the reality of Christian love through the life of this one girl in Tokyo.

When I showed the movie about Miss Kitahara to the students of Sophia University in Tokyo, a non-Christian boy came to me afterward and told me that he would leave his comfortable room at home and move into the slums of Tokyo and work for the children during his free time, to follow the example of this wonderful Christian girl. I know of at least five students who through the example and influence of Miss Kitahara found their way to the Church and are today zealous Christians.

During her short life, Miss Kitahara gave a more powerful witness of Christian love than most Christians give in twice her life-span. Her example may serve as a challenge to people older than she of what they could accomplish by genuine Christian witness. One Christian can, indeed, do a lot to bring Christ and his spirit of love into this world.

François Mauriac, the great Catholic novelist who died in 1970 at the age of eighty-four, wrote before his death his own eulogy in which he said:

> I believe as I did as a child, that life has meaning, a direction, a value; that no suffering is lost, that every tear counts, each drop of blood, that the secret of the world is to be found in Saint John's *"Deus caritas est"*—"God is Love."

Marriage in Old Age:
The New Encounter

For a married couple the time of the husband's retirement can mean a rapid deterioration of their relationship or the beginning of a fuller and richer life together. In some marriages, staying together is only made tolerable by the fact that the husband spends nine hours of each day away from home. In this case, the mere thought that after retirement the man will stay around the home all day can frighten a woman and make her fear the worst. If the retired husband should develop an undue interest in the running of the kitchen and dare to infringe on the domestic domain of his wife, retirement can become sheer hell for the couple, a long series of quarrels and fights, only interrupted by periods of uneasy truce and mutual sullenness.

But a marriage can also take a different turn at the time of retirement, a turn toward a more exalted and intimate relationship. Here, it might be of use to reflect briefly on two different types of interpersonal communication, the latter of which could be an ideal which elderly people might fruitfully try to pursue and to develop more fully. In our achievement- and goal-oriented society most of our communications with other people tend to be of a merely *functional* or useful character. An ordinary business transaction between two people would be an example of such a functional communication. On this level, one person is interchangeable with other human beings. But besides these functional communications there is another type of interpersonal encounter which for lack of a better word we will call *existential* communication. This refers to the deeper experiences of personal relationship which involve a man as an irreplaceable and unique being, and where two people encounter each other and commit themselves to one another as uniquely individual persons. In existential communication no functional goal outside of the true good for both persons is intended; they mutually evoke their potential energies and bring them to full development. In this way both persons, in a sense, create each other.

It would seem that modern society encourages and even forces man during the active years of his life to deal with his fellow men largely on the functional or pre-existential level. Man communicates with man to achieve a common goal, and one person uses the other in the pursuit of this aim. There is, of course, nothing wrong when a man deals with another to achieve objective purposes that lie outside the persons involved. But the danger is that these forms of functional communication become the only ways in which one man meets the other, and this would result in a loss of that dimension in man that is most typically human. One of the more serious dangers of modern civilization lies precisely in its tendency to make the smooth and pleasant yet superficial type of functional dealing with others *the* pattern of all encounters with our fellow men. In this way, men deprive themselves of the in-depth relations that are not primarily geared toward a pleasant and smooth getting-along-with-one-another, but toward confronting one's partner and, through loving strife, chal-

lenging him to develop all the potentialities
of a rich interpersonal relationship. Phi-
losopher-psychologist Karl Jaspers, to whose
insights I am indebted here, has more ex-
tensively developed the enriching possibilities of existential communication and of
loving strife.

The threat of our technology- and
achievement-oriented civilization has to be
met by developing existential communication with other persons. It is essential that
each man reach, in at least some of his
everyday relationships, that depth which
goes beyond the level of the merely functional or useful and meets the other person
at the core of his personality as a nonin-
terchangeable unique individual.

Man should of course, strive for existential communication at each stage of his life
cycle. But old age seems to offer in a special
way both the chance for gaining an understanding for the need of such deeper relationships and the leisure to pursue and
develop them. Freed from the pressure of
functional achievement orientation, man

can newly discover and value those dimensions of life that are most deeply human.

Here we see the possibility of a beautiful venture for a married couple reaching the time of retirement. One of the major tragedies of married life today is that too many husbands and wives even after years of married life still remain on the pre-existential level of communication. All their mutual dealings reflect a merely functional relationship. Thus, a whole rich area of possible human growth and of mutual creation remains undeveloped. One is reminded of C. G. Jung's disquieting remark that man usually works and lives with only half of his psychic potentiality while the other half remains unused and forgotten.

A marriage could become much more enriching if people were made aware of the different levels of personal relations and of the immense possibilities of existential communication. A husband and wife who never reach beyond the merely functional modes of mutual encounter miss the finest chance of their lives. They can hardly be surprised if they experience frustration, boredom, and ultimate dissatisfaction, not to mention a complete breakdown in communication.

A much richer marital relationship could evolve if both partners took up the challenge of existential communication and of loving strife. There is no lack of strife in the average marriage, but often it is not a loving one. On the other hand, many couples think that a kind of love that is free of all difference of opinion is enough and forget that maturation cannot be achieved without the rigor and vigor of a challenging mutual struggle.

Mutual loving criticism of husband and wife does not imply that the partners be an accomplished gentleman and an ideal woman from the onset. In reality, husband and wife are unfinished personalities who only through the process of existential communication gradually evolve into the ideal persons so often wrongly expected to be present from the beginning. Unrealistic presuppositions or expectations can easily ruin a marriage. Husband and wife must seek their task as a mutual creation, where both partners mutually evoke all potential energies and thus lead each other to fulfillment and growth. To strive for this ideal would appear to be a challenging and enriching task for a couple entering the season of "golden age".

Some married couples, especially after all the children are grown, drift away from one another and live almost completely separate lives even though they inhabit the same house. Saint Paul put no time limits on his instruction that "husbands should love their wives just as Christ loved the Church and sacrificed himself for her" (Eph 5:25). Married couples, even old ones, might profitably make the resolution to read Ephesians 5 once a month or so.

New Religious Dimensions

The Christian faith is of such infinite richness that the depth of its truth cannot be fully grasped nor the wealth of its religious and moral values be fully realized at

any given period of man's life. The Gospel
is like an inexhaustible mine of truth and
ideals. The Christian can dig into this mine
year in and year out, but he will never
exhaust it. It is only in the course of suc-
cessive stages in a person's life that the fullness of religious truth gradually reveals
itself and the abundant realm of religious
values can be fully realized by man.

But during each period of man's life,
some unique opportunities are offered him,
possibilities of understanding and acting
that are not given, or at least not to the same
degree, at other stages of life. Sacred Scripture often speaks of a *kairos*, a uniquely
opportune time that comes once and does
not return. Ecclesiastes tells us that everything has its unique time, its *kairos*.

> Everything under the heavens has its
> time. There is a time to be born and a time
> to die, a time for planting and a time for
> uprooting what has been planted . . . a
> time for tears and a time for laughter . . . a
> time for embracing and a time to refrain
> from embracing . . . a time to be silent and
> a time to speak (Qo 3:1–8).

The historicity of man, the fact that man exists and acts only in an historical framework, has been strongly emphasized in contemporary philosophy. Some philosophers seem to be unaware that Sacred Scripture shows a keen sense of man's essentially historical character. Saint Paul writes in his letter to the Romans: "And this is important for us who understand the time of salvation [the *kairos*]: now is the hour to awaken from our sleep" (Rom 13:11). Even the hour of temptation is for the believer a *kairos:* "I will keep you safe in the hour of trial which is coming on the whole world to test those who dwell upon the earth" (Rev 3:10). Repeatedly, Scripture reminds us that, for a man who does not exhaust the given *kairos*, the possibilities of this precious hour will not come back.

God is above time and history, but in his dealings with men he always acts in time and history. "At the appointed time, God revealed his word" (Titus 1:3). At the wedding in Cana, Jesus answers his mother: "My hour has not yet come" (Jn 2:4). Jesus never acts in an autonomous fashion but rather in accordance with the *kairos*, the unique time predetermined and decided by the Father. "My time has not yet come. Your time is always here" (Jn 7:6). "When we were still in misery, Christ, at the set time, died for those who were separated from God" (Rom 5:6). Saint John begins his account of the Last Supper with a very precise statement: "Jesus knew that the hour [the *kairos*] had come for him to pass from this world to the Father" (Jn 13:1).

We are all familiar with the unique opportunities that man's period of youth presents with regard to religious life: a spirit of enthusiasm, of generosity and the possibility of making a magnanimous lifelong commitment in the choice of a vocation.

There seems to be much less awareness of the fact that old age too offers man unique opportunities with regard to his religious life, opportunities that were not given, or at least not to the same degree, during the previous stages of life. Man cannot live his religious and moral life in a nonhistoric manner where he would try to realize religious and moral values independently of the particular period of a given historical life situation. Man must humbly admit that his possibilities are limited at any given time and that each stage of his life cycle presents its own unique *kairos* which will often be different from any previous opportunities of his life.

Unfortunately, many aging men and women get discouraged and depressed by the limitations that old age imposes on them. How much richer could the evening of their life be if they were instead to lift their eyes to the novel horizons of old age! Exploring and discovering the manifold new vistas and opportunities for a more mature religious life can be an exhilarating and rejuvenating experience for an aging person. Later we shall see that, for example, old age seems to grant new possibilities of gaining a deeper understanding of the Trinity and of developing a specifically trinitarian spirituality. Here we will only briefly offer two other examples where old age might open up new dimensions for religion in many lives.

The first example concerns the new discovery of God's strength in human weakness. Aging people are in a unique situation of being able to gain, in their physical decline and diminishment, a new experience of their own finitude and of God's power and might. Each period in man's life offers its own unique opportunities of grasping certain aspects of the infinitely rich reality of the Christian faith. Old age would seem to offer man a new opportunity to develop a deeper confidence and trust in God's providence and grace.

An example from medieval Buddhism may illustrate this point. Hoonen, the founder of the Pure Land School of Buddhism in Japan, taught his followers to trust wholeheartedly in Amida-Buddha and to invoke his holy name. Faith, he said, is the fundamental requisite for a person to be saved. Thanks to the power of faith, Hoonen taught, "even the bad man will be saved; how much more a good man." One of Hoonen's disciples, Shinran, deeply shaken by the experience of human frailty and depravity, reversed Hoonen's doctrine, saying, "even a good man will be saved; how much more a bad one." The point Shinran wanted to bring out in this extreme and paradoxical statement was, of course, that man's actions do not count, neither the good nor the bad ones, but only the saving act of Amida-Buddha.

Without wanting in any way to subscribe to the extreme faith attitude of Shinran's Buddhist school, I am inclined to see in this paradoxical formulation a strong stimulus to search for a more genuine understanding of our frequently inadequate conception of Christian faith and grace. Thus we might be helped to discover the particular dimension of faith that old age could succeed in bringing out. During his active years, the average Christian is inclined to rely primarily on his own strength and to give the main credit for his accomplishments to his own ingenuity and work. To put it in theological jargon, in his more active years man is prone to conceive of grace in a rather Pelagian manner. During this period of his life he often tends to overlook the deep theological truth that he would be nothing and could do nothing without the ever-present sustaining power of God. Once a man grows old and feels how his own strength diminishes, he could well see this as a challenge to gain a deeper understanding of how much his actions and his whole existence are really sustained by the creative and preserving power of Almighty God. Thus, an aging person is offered the new opportunity of experiencing the Christian paradox that, as his own strength declines, the power and glory of God the Creator and Redeemer shines forth ever more brightly in him. Saint Paul expressed this paradox beautifully: "He [Christ] has said, 'My grace is enough for you: my power is at its best in weakness.' So I shall be very happy to make my weaknesses my special boast so that the power of Christ may stay over me, and that is why I am quite content with my weaknesses and with insults, hardships, persecutions and the agonies I go through for Christ's sake. For it is when I am weak that I am strong" (2 Cor 12:9–10).

A second example that can illustrate a

new religious dimension in old age concerns the new awareness of the important values in life and of the great gift of faith. The new detachment from activity enjoyed by an aged person can be a considerable help in gaining the proper perspective on things. It can open one's eyes to the really important values in life and can lead to a joyful rediscovery of the gift of faith. We humans are inclined to take the good things in life for granted. Often we are not even aware that they are gifts we have received from God and for which we ought to be grateful. In old age, when so many previously valued things are called into question, there arises a new sense of what is really important and lasting. Old age sharpens the sense for what is genuine and enduring. Suffering and the decline of health can often open the eyes of a man to lasting values and liberate his spirit for the experience of a deeper happiness.

In this connection, I often think of a leper whom I met in a leprosarium near Tokyo in Japan. On Sundays I went as a chaplain to this leper colony and celebrated Mass for them. There I met an elderly gentleman who had already lost one hand through this terrible disease. To my surprise, he always looked very happy and content. I found out that he was a convert and extremely active as a Catholic, bringing his fellow patients to Mass and trying to spread the glad tidings among his non-Christian co-sufferers. One day I discovered that whereas the majority of lepers were recovering gradually from their sickness, thanks to the progress of modern medicine, and would eventually be able to return home after a few years, this gentleman had no hope at all of ever regaining his health. His leprosy had been discovered too late, and now he was doomed to stay in the leper colony for the rest of his life.

But when I talked with him, far from being gloomy or disheartened, he was always cheerful, and the one dominant theme of his conversations was: "I am so grateful to God that here in the leprosarium I have found the Christian faith, that I have found meaning in my life." He always used the Japanese phrase: "My heart is full of gratitude!" I could not help noticing the stark contrast to the Gospel story about the ten lepers who were healed; nine of them did not even take the time to return and thank Jesus for the miracle. This Japanese leper suffered terrible pain, and yet without physical healing his heart was full of gratitude for the gift that he considered greater than bodily health, his Christian faith.

In a slightly different vein, the religious significance of man's declining years is highlighted in several novels of François Mauriac. Mauriac has depicted the avarice and hatred, the inhumanity and corruption, and the destructive force of man's passions with great poignancy. His works approach the extreme of saying that to live is to sin and that evil is gnawing at the very root of human existence. And yet, in spite of overwhelming human weakness and wickedness, toward the end of their lives Mauriac's great sinners seem to be offered and to accept the gift of grace. Divine grace, for these hauntingly described characters of Mauriac, appears to be most powerfully operative in later life. Only then are their greed, lust and selfishness finally conquered; only then are they liberated from the prison of their isolation and loneliness and led into communion with God and fellow men.

It is only on her deathbed that grace becomes victorious for the heroine of Mauriac's novel *Thérèse*. Mauriac says of Thérèse, "She belongs to that class of human beings [and it is a huge family!] for whom night can end only when life itself ends." *A Kiss for the Leper* is the tragic story of an unhappy marriage between an ugly rich man and a beautiful poor girl. Noémie, the wife, finds her husband's body repulsive. Severe nausea turns her away from him and makes life with him simply repulsive. It is only toward the end, when her husband approaches death, that Noémie discovers his inner beauty and begins truly to love him.

The miserly old landowner in Mauriac's *Vipers' Tangle* chafes under the nagging feeling that nobody loves him. He becomes embittered, and his heart is eaten up by hatred and a desire for revenge, as well as by avarice. Reacting to the cold-heartedness of his family, he decides to take vengeance by disinheriting every one of his relatives. Even in his old age his thoughts and acts are dominated by the spirit of greed, hatred and revenge. It is only in his very last days that glimpses of love which he experiences in some people around him open the heart of this "monster of solitude and indifference". The last entry in the old man's journal culminates in the joyful discovery that finally the icy encasing of avarice and bitterness is melting from around his heart. "Something is making my heart feel as though it would burst—it is the Love whose name at last I know." Writing about the old man after his death, one of his relatives admits that he was a terrible and, at times, a dreadful man. But in spite of this, a great light shone upon him during those last days of his life, and his final goodness entirely changed this relative's outlook on life.

For Mauriac, life seems to be a long and dangerous zigzag course up a steep moun-

tain side. Darkness prevails during most of
the perilous climbing, and the light begins
to glimmer only toward the end when the
sunlit summit emerges in a kind of transcendent way above the uncertain mist of
human existence. Mankind's aspiration
(seldom recognized for what it is) toward
the transcendent Being of God is rarely described so well as it is through Mauriac's
characters.

Sharing in the Life and Love of the Trinity

Many Christians find in their older years a
new understanding of and access to the
central mystery of the Christian faith, the
Blessed Trinity. Sharing in the exchange of
life and love between the three Persons of
the Trinity becomes for some the most creative way to face the loneliness of old age.

We cannot say that the Trinity is a doctrine "for adults only", since it is the very
heart of our faith. But it would seem that
this deepest of Christ's revelations has a
special relevance for mature adults and for

the aging. After having experienced the beauty and the limitations of manifold human relationships, the aged person seems to be particularly prepared for a deeper participation in the perfect exchange of life and love that flows between the three Persons of the Trinity.

When I first taught catechism to non-Christian Japanese in Tokyo, the lesson I was the most anxious about was the one on the Trinity. How could I make intelligible this most difficult and yet most central mystery of the Christian faith to my catechumens, and how would they receive it? I was pleasantly surprised. It was precisely the doctrine of the Trinity that many of my catechumens—especially older ones—found most attractive and meaningful.

Frank Sheed, who often used to speak on the Trinity in London's Hyde Park, has observed the same fascination which the doctrine of the Trinity has for the man in the street, as I found to be the case for my Japanese catechumens in Tokyo. Moreover, he has offered an interesting explanation for this remarkable phenomenon. He compares the fascination which a man experiences from a sudden grasp of the trinitarian mystery to the experience a man has in recognizing a photograph of himself which he has never seen before. He is entranced by the phenomenon of seeing himself (the original) through a copy or reproduction. When a man first learns about the Trinity he undergoes a similar experience, but in reverse. Here, instead of the original recognizing his own image, the image recognizes and is fascinated by the Original.

Having returned for a time to the Christian West, I have often asked myself why the teaching on the Trinity, which in itself has such great appeal, does not play a more central role in the religious awareness, spirituality and moral life of the average Christian. Many teachers and preachers would say: "It is too difficult to explain; and, besides, I do not see the relevance of it."

Yet among all the truths that Christ has revealed to us, none is so profound or far-reaching as this truth about God himself and about man who is created in the image of the triune God. Why should Christ have gone to so much trouble to tell us that there are three Persons in God, unless this truth is of real significance for our Christian life? God certainly did not reveal this truth to provide us with a kind of divine puzzle or to give the catechists who have to struggle to explain this profound mystery a hard time. Rather, God has revealed the mystery of the Trinity to us because it sheds light on our own makeup and the manner in which we should live out our lives, if they are to be significant and fulfilling.

God does not exist as a "loner" or an isolated individual. Rather there is a community within the very being of God. Jesus Christ gives us a glimpse of this profound loving community between the three divine Persons: "The Father loves the Son" (Jn 3:35); "I and the Father are one" (Jn 10:30); "The Father is in me, and I in the Father (Jn 10:38); "The Spirit of truth who proceeds from the Father will be my witness" (Jn 15:26).

The life of God is of its very nature societal. God exists as a fellowship and friendship of three divine Persons. In the Trinity,

each Person has his existence only in relation to the others, and it is only in existing
for the others, in the process of infinite
giving and receiving of love, that each one
is fully himself. The Trinity presents the
highest coincidence of opposites: the highest form of unity coincides with the distinct
selfhood of three divine Persons. Self-being
does not decrease through self-giving, but
rather increases in proportion to the giving
of self. Thus, the Trinity as the source and
model of all personhood and community
shows us that the highest perfection of a
person is not self-assertion, isolation and
independence, but rather openness and
loving commitment to others.

Since the beginning of time, man has
been asking questions about himself and
has gradually built up a wealth of understanding about his own nature and being.
Of all discoveries in man's long search for
self-understanding, however, the most important has been Christ's revolutionary revelation that man is created in the image of a
triune God and that he is "able to share the
divine nature" (2 Pet 1:4). Never in the long

history of the human race has man discovered such an important insight into
himself. Far from being revealed suddenly
and all at once, this tremendous revelation
dawned slowly and in stages. In Genesis it
is reported that God said: "Let us make
man in our image, in the likeness of ourselves" (Gen 1:26). But that God, far from
being a "loner", is a triune God, existing
precisely as a living community of three
divine Persons, and that consequently man
as created in the image of the Trinity possesses within himself a trinitarian structure—this became known to man only
through the revelation of Jesus Christ.

The ethical implications of man's new
Christian understanding of himself as an
image of the Trinity are enormous. Since
God exists, not as a lonely and isolated individual, but in the loving exchange of three
Persons, so man, too, created in the image
of the three-personal God, is at the very
core of his existence a relational being. He
finds his true self and becomes fully human
only in a dialogic relationship of love and
exchange with others.

One immediate consequence of an ethics founded on man's relational nature is the rejection of contemporary Western individualism. There is no more profound refutation of individualism than the fact that man is at the core of his being an image of the God who is in his very essence a community. That God is a tri-personal reality is, then, the ultimate foundation and origin of all human community. God wills community for man because he himself exists as community and has created man in his own trinitarian image. This same principle explains why Jesus Christ is so radical in his demands regarding love of neighbor. Since man is structured in the likeness of the Trinity, with its interpersonal fullness of life, he is ordained to living out a life of loving communication with his fellow men at the deepest level of his being.

In the first chapter of this book we saw that our Western civilization overemphasized the independence and autonomy of the individual and neglected the values of solidarity and community. We are all aware how rapidly our society is disintegrating because of untrammeled individualism. The aged who are suffering most from the burden of isolation and loneliness have a great desire to overcome the atomization of society and find a new sense of community.

The urgency of this problem has recently been stressed by social scientists and theologians alike. Sociologist Philip Slater, for example, in *The Pursuit of Loneliness* has analyzed the social and psychological forces that are pulling American society apart. According to Slater, the three human desires —the desires for community, engagement and dependence—are uniquely frustrated by American culture. An extreme individualism is at the root of most of America's present perplexities. Since "a prepotent individualism is not a viable foundation for any society in a nuclear age", we must overcome this untrammeled individualism and develop a new sense of community.

Working to bring together the isolated and lonely old people would seem to be a genuine moral imperative for our society. We have to find ways to throw off our present individualism and to build new communities if we really want to provide a humane and Christian way of life for our old people.

An understanding of man in the light of the Trinity offers an important answer to the present search for community. This trinitarian anthropology emphasizes that man is a radically communitarian being. The Trinity shows us that community is of the very essence of God. God is not a lonely person; rather, there is a community within the very Being of God. This supreme divine community is the ultimate model of all forms of community. In the Trinity, each person exists only in his relation to the others, and it is only in existing for the others, in the process of infinite giving and receiving of love, that each one is fully himself.

Being created according to the image of this trinitarian God-as-community, the human person, too, is essentially a being-in-community. Man is not first an individualist and then secondarily a social being. Rather, man is in his very nature directed toward the "thou" of other persons and can become fully himself and fully human only through the dynamic process of imitating in a human community the mutual giving and receiving of love that exists between the three Persons in the Trinity. Everything that hinders man from being fully available to other persons prevents him at the same time from being fully himself.

Older people have more leisure for meditation and prayer. A meditative approach to the triune God can become a most enriching experience for aging man. In the process of meditative sharing in the inner trinitarian life and love, the Trinity reveals itself to man as Father, Son and Holy Spirit and offers him a glimpse of the infinite richness and beauty of the three-personed community of love. As man lets himself be drawn and immersed into the ebb and flow of the powerful life movement flowing between the three divine Persons, the touch of infinite life makes him come alive in a radically new way.

A meditative participation in the life of the Trinity now here on earth will make us ever more aware that the risen Christ is present in us, instilling already now into the aging body the new divine life and love that will never age or diminish. Such contemplative sharing in the Trinity will nourish an ever growing yearning and desire for a fuller consummation of this exchange of love. It will create a new eschatological desire among Christians which we find so vividly expressed in the early Church, "We groan as we wait with longing to enter our heavenly home" (2 Cor 5:2).

To the extent that we are drawn into the intimacy of God's own trinitarian life and love, our desire for a more total union will increase. It is like the experience of two young lovers who have tasted the beauty of their tender feelings for each other and are then powerfully drawn to the full consummation of marital love. If the mighty ebb and flow of the eternal trinitarian life has touched man, then an insatiable yearning arises in him to be fully encompassed by it and to share ever more deeply in this greatest community of love in the Trinity.

Old age can become an enriching experience if it leads man to a fuller participation in the ideal interpersonal relationship of infinite self-giving and infinite reception of love that we witness in the Trinity. In the Trinity we find the perfect prototype of that which all genuine love between persons reaches out restlessly to obtain: to be one with the other, and yet in this communion not to lose one's identity but to discover it. The Trinity shows us that the beautiful paradox is possible: the more you give yourself to the beloved, the more you become the person you really are. Aging man can reach a new undreamed-of depth of I-Thou encounter if he allows himself to be received into the dynamic stream of life and love that flows between the three Persons of the Trinity. This sharing in the trinitarian love can unlock in man an infinite new energy of love that perhaps has so far lain dormant, waiting to be stirred up and enkindled.

Besides being a profound answer to the problem of loneliness in old age, a deeper sharing in the love of the Trinity will also initiate a dialectical process of simultaneous growth of one's relationship to God and toward one's fellow men. That is, the more deeply man enters into the sublime dialogue of loving God and sharing in the exchange of love among the three divine Persons, the more he becomes capable of giving himself in service and love to others.

Our occupation in heaven for all eternity will consist in a profound participation in the interpersonal love of Father, Son and Holy Spirit. This in turn disposes us for a deeper encounter with our fellow men in heaven. Trying to enter more deeply into this perfect dialogue of love in the Trinity would be for aging man an ideal initiation and anticipation of his eternal future.

"I Am Going to the Father"

Coming to terms with the inescapable fact of approaching death is one of the tasks of every aging person. It is often amazing how immature some old people can be when it comes to such a basic fact as death. I remember one seventy-year-old man who was so frightened by it that he ran out of the room whenever the word death was mentioned. One day I gave him the beautiful letter that Mozart wrote about death at the age of thirty-one. The old man told me later that he was ashamed about his attitude and changed it when he saw how it contrasted with the mature way with which Mozart, a man less than half his age, approached his impending death. Four years before his death at thirty-five, Mozart wrote to his father:

> Since death [to be precise] is the true end purpose of our life, I have made it my business over the past few years to get to know this true, this best, friend of man so well that the thought of him not only holds no terrors for me but even brings me great comfort and peace of mind. I thank my God that he has granted me the good fortune and opportunity to get to know death as the key to our true happiness. I never go to bed without reflecting on the thought that perhaps, as young as I am, the next day I might not be alive anymore. And no man who knows me will be able to say that in social intercourse I am morose or sad. For this happiness I thank every

day my Creator, and with all my heart I
wish this happiness for all my fellowmen
(written April 4, 1787).

Feeling that his life was to end soon,
Mozart reached at the age of thirty-one a
mature and even joyful attitude toward
death, an attitude which takes many people
seventy years to achieve.

Many Christians have too narrow a view
of life after death, thinking of heaven ex-
clusively in terms of "eternal rest" and "vision of God". These two conceptions,
although valid in a limited sense, tend to
distort the genuine meaning of eternal life
by conveying a rather negative and passive
view of heaven. In the light of a trinitarian
spirituality one would see heaven and eternal life as the highest creative possibility of
man: actively participating in the ultimate
life and love of the three divine Persons and
in their creativity. The terms "eternal rest"
and "beatific vision" retain their limited va-
lidity: we will indeed "rest" insofar as there
will be no tiring and boring labor or any
dull and wearying activity; and there will

be an enriching "vision" of God, for the Trinity is of inexhaustible beauty. But the emphasis should not be on the negative and passive side but rather on the joyous celebration of the eternal banquet in personal communion with the Father, Son and Holy Spirit and with the whole community of saints transformed in love.

Our present existence on earth and eternal life in heaven must be seen in close continuity. The mystical sharing in the trinitarian life here on earth and our loving self-gift to other persons will thus become a preparation and training of that activity which will be man's eternal occupation in heaven: sharing creatively in the trinitarian self-giving and reception of love between Father, Son and Holy Spirit in union with our fellow human beings.

Some people frown upon the idea of turning one's mind toward the future life in heaven. They say that this is only an escape from man's responsibility here on earth. In some cases, thinking of heaven might indeed be an escape from a situation where man should concentrate on solving a problem here on earth. But in old age, man may sometimes reach a point where there is no great task to be fulfilled anymore here on earth, where a man has done his life's work and reached the point of unbearable loneliness and pain. A person who is suffering from terminal cancer, for example, has not much to look forward to in this life.

If man reaches a moment like this where the earthly life offers no prospect and hope for brighter days, it is good to have at hand some Scripture texts that describe the joys and consolations of our future life in heaven.

One such text is in the discourse of Christ during the Last Supper: "Do not let your hearts be troubled. Trust in God still, and trust in me. There are many rooms in my Father's house; if there were not, I should have told you. I am going to prepare a place for you, and after I have gone and prepared you a place, I shall return to take you with me; so that where I am you may be too" (Jn 14:1–3). Another beautiful description of the future life in heaven can be found in the Book of Revelation: "They will never hunger or thirst again; neither the sun nor scorching wind will ever plague them, because the Lamb who is at the throne will be their shepherd and will lead them to springs of living water: and God will wipe away all tears from their eyes" (Rev 7:16–17).

Saint Paul emphasizes that the beauty and harmony of heaven will be far beyond anything we have seen or heard: "The things that no eye has seen and no ear has heard, things beyond the mind of man, all that God has prepared for those who love him" (1 Cor 2:9). Writing the Apocalypse on the island of Patmos, Saint John was overwhelmed with the joy and happiness of the future life: "Then I heard a voice from heaven say to me, 'Write down: Happy are those who die in the Lord! Happy indeed, the Spirit says; now they can rest forever after their work, since their good deeds go with them'" (Rev 14:13). Finally, here is a simple, yet moving thought from Saint Paul: "So we shall always be with the Lord. Comfort one another with these words" (1 Th 4:17).

Crossing the Desert into the Promised Land

Growing old in a positive way is like crossing the desert into the promised land. Aging makes man aware how unstable and transient so many things in life are. Wealth and external achievements, beauty and health: all are fleeting and perishable. But experiencing the transient nature of things is only one side of the coin. The aging man also develops a new awareness of the lasting and the eternal. In the midst of diminishing human life, man can acquire a newly deepened faith in the never-ending eternal life in union with the triune God. The dimension of the eternal future reveals itself as a warm and splendid light that illuminates the present and gives a new meaning and hope to it all.

Although a man knows that he still has to pass through the gate of suffering and death, he knows too that this final, all-important step will be a sharing in the suffering and death of Jesus Christ, a transition toward the resurrection and eternal life with the glorious risen Christ in the Trinity.

Man will now see his aging process as an important stage of generous self-giving, of growth and completion which finds its culmination in the total union with the suffering, dying and rising Christ.

Growing old means to this man a painful and yet glorious crossing of the desert on the journey into the promised land, a land not of inert eternal "rest", but of the most joyful, loving friendship with Christ in the Blessed Trinity.

MAN'S IMMORTALITY
AND ETERNAL LIFE

*The Problem of Immortality—Can Life Be
Meaningful If It Ends with Death?*

In his book *La Condition humaine*,[1] André
Malraux records a pessimistic conversation
between a husband and wife:

> Listen, May, it does not take nine months
> to make a man, it takes fifty years—fifty
> years of sacrifice, of determination, of—so
> many things. And when that man has
> been achieved, when there is no child-
> ishness left in him, or any adolescence,
> when he is truly, utterly, man—the only
> thing he is good for is to die.

[1] André Malraux, *La condition humaine* (Paris:
Gallimard, 1946), 403; English version, *Man's Fate*
(New York: Random House, 1961), 282.

In this bitter remark, Malraux expresses the futility of life. If human death has no meaning, then man's life becomes meaningless.

The film *Zorba the Greek*, based on the novel by Nikos Kazantzakis, raises the issue in an even more poignant way. A young widow on a small Greek island is condemned to death because she has spurned the attentions of a young man of the island in favor of a handsome visiting Englishman, thus contributing to the suicide of the disappointed native. After her execution, Zorba asks the young Englishman who had loved the murdered girl: "Why do young people die? Why does anybody die? Don't your books and all your study tell you that?" After a long pause the Englishman answers: "My books only tell about the agony of not being able to answer questions like yours." Zorba replies: "I spit on your agony."

One can sympathize with Zorba the Greek. If all our books and all our learning cannot tell us anything about death and its meaning, what good are they? If we do not know death, we cannot know life. If there is no meaning in death, how can there be meaning in life?

Death is a fact of life which no one can ignore and a fate which no one can escape. However, whether or not a man sees a meaning in death and whether or not there is the possibility of a life after death greatly affects man's present life—either threatening him with a sense of futility or filling man's heart with hope, expectation and optimism even in the midst of suffering and death.

There is probably no single argument which can offer a clear proof that man will live on after death. However, in the long history of mankind, many different approaches toward the immortality of man have been found, and together they offer a convergence of probabilities. I shall first briefly delineate seven of these typical approaches and describe the convergence of their probabilities. Then we will reflect on what such a possible life after death may be like. Finally, we will consider what meaning a belief in a life after death could have for our present life today.

Seven Approaches to the Question of Immortality

1. Socrates and Plato: man's soul is essentially immortal

One of the most impressive proponents of a life after death in the history of philosophy is Socrates. What appeals particularly to us in the twentieth century is the fact that Socrates did not present his theory of man's immortality in an ivory tower of mere academic learning; rather, he literally sacrificed his earthly life in order to impress on his disciples his strong conviction that what is essential in man will live on after death. Even during the last hours before his death, Socrates did not lose his self-composure but cheerfully spoke of his new life that would start at the moment of death.[2]

Socrates' disciple Plato has given us a classical statement of the philosophical idea of immortality in his book *Phaedo*[3] where he describes the last days of Socrates. For both Socrates and Plato, the human soul is essentially indestructible. At the time of death, the soul of a good man departs from the body to a new existence of complete happiness. Throughout his whole life, man is a seeker after truth, but his body and the material world that surrounds him allow him only a partial view of truth and reality. Death offers man a full view of truth, and is, therefore, a moment of fulfillment of all his yearnings, indeed, a happy event. Socrates can thus approach the hour of death with serene hope and expectation of fulfillment.

The dualistic view of man with its sharp contrast between body and soul and the

[2] Plato, "Phaedo", in *The Collected Dialogues of Plato* (New York: Pantheon Books, 1966), 40–98.

[3] Ibid.

rather negative evaluation of the body are not in tune with our present-day interpretation of man as a psychosomatic unity. Nevertheless, Plato's teaching that the core of man is indestructible and is destined for an immortal life portrays a grand vision of the dignity of man that has exercised a strong appeal to philosophers in subsequent generations.

2. The historical fact of belief in afterlife in all peoples, cultures and ages

A second argument for man's immortality is the historical fact that the idea of immortality has been alive in all cultures and in all ages, in ancient Egypt as well as in modern America, among primitive African tribes and Alaskan Eskimos, among Indian Hindus as well as among Japanese Shintoists and Buddhists. The Egyptian *Book of the Dead*, which dates from around 3500 B.C. and is considered by some scholars to be the oldest book of mankind, describes the journey of the human soul into eternal life as a factual certainty. The magnificent pyramids of Egypt bear witness to the strong conviction of a life after death among the ancient Egyptians. American Indian tribes strongly emphasize the deep spiritual unity of the living and the dead. The *Tibetan Book of the Dead* intends to prepare a person for death and guide him to a new existence of rebirth in paradise. The Koran, the basic book of Islam, offers vivid descriptions of the joyful life awaiting the good person after death. A famous African poem ends with the verse "The dead are never dead", expressing the typical conviction of African tribes. Belief in an afterlife is, however, not restricted to past historical ages or to primitive tribes. According to a 1975 Gallup poll, 69 percent of all Americans believe there is life after death, 20 percent do not believe it, while 11 percent said they don't know.

Within this general pattern of mankind's strong interest in life after death, Japan is, of course, no exception. The annual *Obon* celebrations indicate a conviction that one's ancestors are not completely extinguished with death. The traditional ancestor worship expresses a certain communitarian bond between the deceased and the living. The *kamidana* or the *butsudan* occupy a central place in many Japanese homes. It is here that the family keeps the memory of the departed family members alive and cultivates a sense of closeness between the living and the dead. The mortuary tablet *(ihai)* also suggests a belief that death is not a total annihilation of the departed ones.

The historical fact that belief in an afterlife is nearly universal among all peoples shows that such a belief is deep-seated in human nature.

3. Human potential and man's infinite task: James, Kant, Goethe

A third argument for immortality takes its starting point from man's enormous human potential and his infinite moral task. During most of his lifetime, the American philosopher William James did not show any interest in the question of immortality. But during the last few years of his life he began to believe in its possibility. When asked why, he said, "Because I am just becoming fit to live." Like James, many people feel in the later years of their life that so many of their talents have been developed slowly over many years and now that they have finally become masters there must be a chance to write better books, to paint vaster portraits and to sing more beautiful songs transcending the approaching moment of death. Otherwise, life as a whole would appear such an enormous waste, a road without a goal.

For the German philosopher Immanuel Kant, the doctrine of immortality is a "postulate of practical reason". In his *Critique of Practical Reason*,[4] he shows that we are required by moral law to be perfect. However, during the limited time of our earthly existence, we are not capable of fulfilling the demand of this moral law. According to Kant, an obligation is invalid unless it can be fulfilled. Man can fulfill his grand moral task only in an endless progress from lower to higher stages of moral perfection. This infinite progress is possible only if man's

[4] Kant, *Kritik der praktischen Vernunft*, pt. 1, vol. 2, bk. 2. Haupstück, IV.

existence extends beyond death, in other words, if man's soul is immortal.

The poet Goethe speaks repeatedly of the immortality of man. He bases his conviction of man's eternity on the "entelechy" inherent in man's nature, a dynamic force which is now present as a potential but which strives for full actualization beyond death.[5] According to Goethe, the human spirit is of an undestructible nature. He compares the death of man to the setting of the sun. To the human eye the setting sun seems to disappear, but in reality it continues to shine with equal splendor.[6] Goethe also stresses the relevancy of belief in eternal life for our present existence. "I would say that those who have no hope for a future life are already dead for the present one."[7] It is no wonder then that *Faust*, Goethe's greatest literary creation, ends with the vision of Faust's eternal salvation.

[5] Eckermann, *Gespräche mit Goethe* (Zurich: Artemis, 1948), 371.

[6] Ibid., May 2, 1824.

[7] Ibid., February 2, 1829.

4. Gabriel Marcel's philosophy of love, death and immortality

One of the most original arguments for a life after death was proposed by the existentialist philosopher Gabriel Marcel. Whereas other thinkers usually take their own death as the starting point of their reflections, Marcel envisages, not his own death, but the death of the person he loves. For Marcel the problem of death is essentially the conflict between love and death. "What matters is neither my death nor yours; it is the death of the one we love."[8] According to Marcel, one cannot truly love without wishing immortality for the loved one.

In his analysis of love, Marcel shows that genuine love always includes the hope and desire that this love and the loved partner will last for all eternity. Love that is satisfied with temporal limitation cannot be genuine, for love always means "forever".

Perhaps one of the most beautiful for-

[8] Gabriel Marcel, *Présence et Immortalité* (Paris: Flammarion, 1959), 182.

mulations about the mystery of love and death is Marcel's famous words: "To love a being is to say, 'Thou, thou shalt not die'." For Marcel this sentence is no mere wish. The loving relationship between the I and the Thou is essentially indestructible. If death would simply annihilate our love and loved partner, love and the I-Thou relationship would ultimately lose its most profound meaning. The death of the loved one is the ultimate test of the profundity of our love when we discover how deep our love really is. If we were to equate the death of the loved one with his final annihilation, we would according to Marcel, "betray" this love, whereas the conviction of the loved one's immortality is genuine "fidelity".

The conflict of love and death found a classical expression in the ancient myth of Orpheus and Eurydice, in which Orpheus descended into the realm of the dead to search and regain his beloved Eurydice. Marcel writes in a journal entry of May 10, 1943, that the myth of Orpheus and Eurydice is at the heart of his existence. He adds, "The existential problem has always been and still is for me to know how we can meet again."[9]

In the final words of his book *Homo Viator*, written in the death-filled days of World War II in Paris, Marcel invokes courage and a spirit of preparedness for the great journey towards eternity:

Oh, spirit of metamorphosis!

When we try to obliterate the frontier of clouds which separates us from the other world guide our unpracticed movements! And, when the given hour shall strike, arouse us, eager as the traveller who straps on his backpack while beyond the misty windowpane the earliest rays of dawn are faintly visible.[10]

5. Life as a continuous process of dying and being born: many little deaths— many little births; great death—great birth

[9] Ibid., 132.
[10] *Homo Viator* (New York: Harper & Row, 1962), 270.

Many poets and philosophers have used the image that dying is a kind of being born.[11] It was common among the early Christians to call the day of their death their birthday. This image is based on the common human experience that throughout our lives death and birth repeat themselves. For the baby, the process of being born must appear like the process of dying. The mother's womb is for the fetus a genuine home; the process of being born appears like being forcibly expelled from a warm and comfortable home into a cold and unknown world. Man's whole life then becomes a series of little deaths and little births. He dies to a small world and is born into a larger one. Separation from the mother's womb gives man his independence as an individual person; he is born as a unique person. Separation from the mother's breast is again like a small death through which man is born into a new world of selfhood. When entering kindergarten, the small child loses the protective

[11] Peter J. Kreeft, *Love Is Stronger than Death* (San Francisco: Harper & Row, 1979), 62–69.

home atmosphere and has to be born into a new world where he has to search for his own place. Moving away from one's school, neighborhood or city, saying good-bye to friends, parents, teachers, these are all many small deaths through which man is born again and again into a new larger world of his own making. All human separation in later life, the loss of a friend, the loss of one's husband or wife are like little deaths. But through the pain and suffering of separation a new I is being born. One may also compare this lifelong process of dying and being born again to a multistage rocket. Each stage of the rocket falls away and dies when its job is done. Its job was only to launch the rocket forward to the next stage of life. If thus our whole life is a series of little deaths and little births, one can naturally wonder whether the great death at the end of our life does not also signify birth pangs of a great birth. All the small deaths during our life then become symbols and preparatory stages of the great death which signifies birth into eternal life, when all the little births and little deaths cease forever, a timeless and spaceless for-ever.

6. A poetic vision of eternal life by a novelist who died young (Thomas Wolfe)

People who are close to death often seem to possess a delicate antenna that can pick up wavelengths that are not accessible to ordinary people. Not only do their ears hear a special message from the realm awaiting them beyond death, their eyes seem to see a vision to which ordinary people are blind.

The American novelist Thomas Wolfe, whose language is famous for its extraordinary lyrical power, died in 1938 at the young age of not quite thirty-eight years. During most of his lifetime he was not a religious man, and yet shortly before his early death he wrote one of the most beautiful pictures of encountering God at the moment of death. Since these verses are so different from everything else he had written before, they seem to originate from a profound interior experience. Thomas Wolfe was a genius with words. These are the last words of his last book, *You Can't Go Home Again*, his poetic testament, so to speak, describing his splendid vision of the eternal life awaiting the young poet after death:

Dear Fox, old friend, thus we have come to the end of the road that we were to go together. My tale is finished—and so farewell.

But before I go, I have just one more thing to tell you:

Something has spoken to me in the night, burning the tapers of the waning year; something has spoken in the night, and told me I shall die, I know not where. Saying:

"To lose the earth you know, for greater knowing; to lose the life you have, for greater life; to leave the friends you loved, for greater loving; to find a land more kind than home, more large than earth—

"—Whereon the pillars of this earth are founded, toward which the conscience of the world is tending—a wind is rising, and the rivers flow."[12]

[12] Thomas Wolfe, *You Can't Go Home Again* (New York: Harper & Brothers, 1940), 743.

7. Scientific evidence for afterlife from deathbed observations and reports of resuscitated patients (Osis and Moody)

Probably the most scientific research on the experience of dying patients has been done by Dr. Karlis Osis and Erlendur Haraldsson. After twenty years of research they published in 1977 the book *At the Hour of Death*.[13]

In 1959 Dr. Osis sent a questionnaire to ten thousand doctors and nurses asking for information about visionary experiences they had observed among dying patients. About three thousand deathbed visions and experiences of an unusual nature were then scientifically evaluated. Between 1961 and 1964 Osis conducted a second survey in the United States, and in 1972–73, together with Dr. Haraldsson, a similar research in India. All reports were done by doctors and nurses who were in close contact with dying patients and who were trained in objective reporting. They investi-

[13] Karlis Osis and Erlendur Haraldsson, *At the Hour of Death* (New York: Avon, 1977).

gated mainly three experiences at the time of death: apparitions or experiences of other human beings or nonhuman beings, visions of places apparently not known to the physical senses of the dying patients and elevations of mood or experiences of elation at death. The cross-cultural check of the research in the U.S. and India showed an amazing similarity of experiences in dying patients of such diverse cultural, educational and religious background. From among the vast research results, the following points are of particular interest: apparitions of relatives, friends or of some superhuman or divine being occurred often shortly before death. Fear of death usually ceased, the pain of sickness often disappeared, instead, the patients frequently experienced a new sense of well-being and even joy. Many patients claimed to "see" into the beyond shortly before dying. This deathbed vision revealed to them a new world of light, beauty and intense color. The experience of this vision and of meeting and talking to previously deceased persons who were waiting for them transformed the patients. The experience brought serenity, peace, elation and religious emotion. The patients were freed from fear, pain and gloom and died a "good death", their hearts filled with hope for a future life.

A typical example from the thousands of deathbed experiences is that of a sixteen-year-old American girl who had just come out of a coma. Her consciousness was very clear when she said to the respondent:

> "I can't get up", and she opened her eyes. I raised her a little bit and she said, "I see him, I see him. I am coming." She died immediately afterwards with a radiant face, exultant, elated".[14]

Dr. Osis adds this comment:

> What could possibly make a sixteen-year-old girl "exultant" and "radiant" when giving up a life still unfulfilled? The shortened span of years did not seem to matter. We will see this same, inexplicable fascination with an unseen "something" again and again. The same patients who were in

14 Ibid., 34–35.

pain, who were miserable and scared, seemed to take a peek at the "other-world" reality and become "exultant" and "radiant"—eager to go into it.[15]

Osis does not claim that he has a strict "proof" for a life after death. But his twenty years of research and the evidence based on observations by more than a thousand doctors and nurses lead him to the conviction that "this evidence strongly suggests life after death. . . . Taken in conjunction with other evidence obtained by competent research into this question, we feel that the total body of information makes possible a fact-based, rational and therefore realistic belief in life after death."[16]

Whereas Osis' book is a highly scientific research report, filled with charts and statistical data, Raymond Moody, a medical doctor and psychiatrist, has published a popular book based on interviews with about fifty people who had a near-death experience, some of whom had been de-

[15] Ibid.
[16] Ibid., 3.

clared medically dead and were later re-suscitated. After publishing *Life after Life*[17] in 1975, Moody received hundreds of letters describing similar experiences. Out of this material Dr. Moody compiled a second book, *Reflections on Life after Life*.[18] Moody's findings are for the most part in harmony with those of Dr. Osis. However, his case studies are far richer in detail and offer more colorful descriptions of the patients' experiences after they had been declared medically dead. Here are a few characteristic experiences: almost everyone emphasized that human words cannot adequately express the afterlife experience. Many report hearing themselves declared dead by the doctor. The pain disappeared; they felt a sense of incredible peace and harmony. Many patients tell of hearing some kind of noise, of being drawn through a dark, tunnel-like space. Then they were separated from their bodies and were able

[17] Raymond Moody, *Life after Life* (Atlanta: Mockingbird Books, 1975).

[18] Raymond Moody, *Reflections on Life after Life* (Atlanta: Mockingbird Books, 1977).

to observe their bodies from the outside. Many describe their coming into the presence of "a being of light", whom some identify more concretely as Jesus or God. A review of the person's entire life was also reported by a good number of people.

People with a near-death experience seem to have lost their fear of death because they glimpsed a new meaningful and more beautiful life beyond death. They seem to have gained a deeper sense of human values, of love, of time and eternity. They seem to have discovered a new sense of purpose and meaning in their daily lives. For them, death is no longer the extinction of life but rather the entrance into a new and better form of existence.

Dr. Elisabeth Kübler-Ross, whose book *On Death and Dying*[19] stimulated much of the recent research in thanatology, said in a public statement that her data of research with dying patients convinced her "beyond the shadow of a doubt" that an afterlife does indeed exist.

[19] Elisabeth Kübler-Ross, *On Death and Dying* (New York: Macmillan, 1969).

Seven Approaches to
the Question of Immortality

Several approaches to the immortality of
man, from the philosophical reflections of
Socrates to the scientific inquiries of Osis,
have been considered. I do not claim that
any of the above approaches offers a strict
scientific "proof" of life after death. However, each offers some probability, and, together, they present a convergence of
probabilities. The viewpoints considered all
had different starting points and different
methodologies: metaphysical, psychological, existential, poetic reflections, as well as
scientific data-based and computer-evalu-
ated research. But all approaches reached
the same conclusion, namely, the probability that man will live on after death. This
convergence of probabilities can be illus-
trated by the following chart:

What does this convergence of probabilities mean for our concrete daily life? A
look at our reaction to other probabilities
may be helpful. If I am mortally sick and a
doctor tells me that this sickness will prob-

Eternal life after death—immortality

convergence of
probabilities:

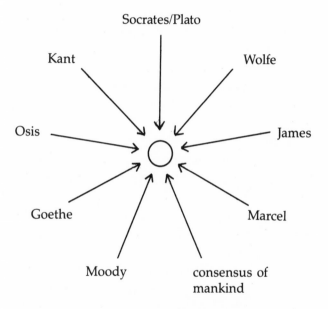

ably kill me within a week if I do not do
anything about it, but that there is a high
probability that I will live if I have an operation, would it not be reasonable to agree to
an operation even if there is no absolute

certainty that the operation will be successful? A high probability with regard to immortality means that it would be unreasonable to ignore the possibility that I may live on after death. In fact, it would seem reasonable to become intensely interested, indeed curious, about this possible eternal future and make it an integral part of my whole thinking about life. If there is a prospect of eternal life, life itself can take on a whole new dimension of hope and optimism.

During the last hour before his death, Socrates spoke of the belief in immortality as a "noble risk" that is worth taking. "Since we have clear evidence that the soul is immortal, this, I think, is both a reasonable contention and a belief worth risking, for the risk is a noble one."[20] Some translators render Plato's expression as "a beautiful risk". Even if a strict proof for the immortality of man is not possible, the high probability based on a convergence of numer-

20 Plato, "Phaedo", 114 d 3–5.

ous probabilities can offer man a reasonable certainty. Basing one's hopes and planning one's life on this conviction would seem to be a "beautiful risk".

The Theological Approach to Immortality as a Confirmation of the Philosophical Hypothesis

In the foregoing reflections we restricted our attention to the insights of human reason. For the Christian believer, the conviction of immortality gained from philosophical and scientific arguments is confirmed by the revelation of God. The Christian believes that God has revealed himself through Jesus Christ. The Bible is considered to be the message of God. Jesus Christ and the Bible confirm the view that man, indeed, has been called to live an eternal life of happiness beyond death. The basic argument of Christian theology for the eternal dimension of man is the fact that man is loved by the eternal love of God; and if God truly loves man he cannot allow him to be annihilated in death. Man can no longer totally perish because he is loved by God.[21] All love by its very nature desires eternity, but God's infinite love not only wants man's eternity, Almighty God also has the power to effect an eternal life beyond death.

According to the Christian understanding of the human person, man has become a dialogue partner of God. Through Jesus Christ, God himself has opened the dialogue of love with man. The basic structure of the whole New Testament message is God's call and man's response. If man answers the call of God, he becomes a permanent partner in the dialogue of love between God and man. Since the love of God as revealed in Jesus Christ is an infinite love it cannot be a mere temporal dialogue that would end one day. When the eternal God starts a loving dialogue with man, this dialogue is by its very nature a neverending love. The eternal love of God offers, therefore, a strong basis of confidence in life

[21] Joseph Ratzinger, "Jenseits des Todes", in Alfons Rosenberg (ed.), *Leben nach dem Sterben* (München: Kösel, 1974), 26–27, 30–31.

after death. Being called and loved by God and responding to this call and love, man begins already here on earth to participate in the infinity and eternity of God himself.

In the light of Christian revelation we can extend the above chart as follows:

revelation of God, Bible, about the eternal life of man

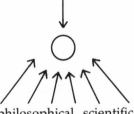

philosophical, scientific
hypothesis (convergence of probabilities)

What Is Eternal Life?

1. Eternal life as a continuous process of transformation, self-realization and growth—man's infinite potentiality

A painful experience that awakened in me an intense interest in man's fate after death was the sudden unexpected death of a brilliant friend of mine at the young age of thirty. He had invested all his years in hard study and was just emerging as a promising young scholar. After finishing his doctorate he was finally ready to start his academic career. Just at the dawn of his scholarly life, he was run over by a car while walking to the library and instantly killed. All the years of his life he had prepared himself for the great work, and precisely when his lifework was to begin, his life ended. In the painful days of mourning my friend's death I kept asking myself: Can all the promising potential of my friend's life that remained undeveloped here on earth be wasted forever? If all his unfulfilled possibilities were completely wasted, would not life be absurd?

Ever since this painful experience the question keeps troubling me: What about all the enormous human potential that remains unused, undeveloped, unrealized in our short lifetime? Even if my friend had lived for seventy years, only a fragment of his brilliant possibilities could have been realized. I shall never forget the words of an elderly gentlemen who told me on his seventy-fifth birthday: "How small a part of my lifework have I been able to carry out. After a lifetime of study and hard work I finally feel ready for a grand life project. But now death is already waiting around the corner."

For all of us, a great part of our possibilities, probably the greater part of our human potential, remains unused and undeveloped. The Swiss psychologist C. G. Jung claims that the average person develops not more than half of his or her potential. William James estimates that a human being is usually functioning at less than 10 percent of his capacity. Many American scientists who have explored the human potential all reach the same conclusion, namely, that man is using a very small fraction of his capacities. Margaret Mead quotes a 6 percent figure; Herbert Otto's estimate is 5 percent or even less.[22]

Discovering our hidden potentials and activating them is one of the most challenging tasks of our lifetime. Personality growth occurs through self-actualization. The full

[22] Herbert A. Otto (ed.), *Human Potentialities* (St. Louis: Green, 1968).

development of man's capacities—especially the capacity for love, creativity, spiritual experience, joy and humor—are an unending process throughout life. But since man's creative capacities are nearly infinite, they cannot be fully exhausted during the limited time of this earthly life. Naturally, the question arises whether this creative process of continuous self-realization should not be continued beyond the moment of death. If not, man and the whole project of man's life and noble endeavors would end as an unfinished torso.

For me, one of the most attractive images of eternal life in heaven is the continuous process of self-realization. In other words, heaven means a continuous actualization of the infinite potential that lies in us and waits to be realized. In this way we shall be gradually transformed until we become the kind of persons that we always wanted to be. In an eternal process we shall always find new visions, discover new potentials and move toward new goals. With each new stage of self-realization we shall discover new dimensions of what it means to be a full human person.

This transformation and self-realization occur, of course, always in loving dialogue with other persons who go through the same process of personality growth. The self-transformation and dynamic self-realization are an important source of eternal happiness, but equally important as a source of happiness are the loving encounter and dialogue with other persons.

In the Christian interpretation of eternal life, in heaven we will be both with the people we love and with God who meets us with infinite love. Since God himself as well as his love are infinite, our encounter with God opens up a dynamic process of infinite growth in love. The partner of our eternal love is infinite, therefore, we can participate to a certain degree in infinity.

2. Eternal life according to the New Testament

In depicting the happiness of eternal life Jesus freely uses different images according to the audience he is addressing. Talking to the Samaritan woman he speaks of "life-giving water and eternal life" (Jn 4:3). For traders he compares heaven to a "precious pearl" for the sake of which it is worthwhile selling everything (Mt 13:45). Again, in addressing himself to the general public, Jesus uses another image that probably had the strongest appeal to the people of Palestine at that time: heaven is like a wedding feast, like an eternal banquet (Mt 22:1–14).

Jesus chose different descriptions and promised his listeners their eternal happiness under the images that most appealed to them as they were. In this way, Jesus evidently wants to encourage us to use our imagination freely when thinking about heaven. We should have no hesitation in depicting heaven with the features that appeal most to us. Twentieth-century Japanese may not necessarily feel attracted by the same features that Palestinians found appealing two millennia ago. The implicit message of Jesus seems to be: feel free to use your creative imagination! Whatever means genuine and deep happiness to you, that will be given to you in heaven. But the happiness of heaven will always transcend anything we can dream of with our limited human imagination.

As a small child cannot possibly understand the happiness and joy of a mature husband-wife relationship in marriage, so we cannot yet at this stage fully grasp the bliss of heaven that is awaiting us beyond death. Saint Paul points out that eternal life will be a new experience beyond anything we can know here on earth. He speaks of "the things that no eye has seen and no ear has heard, things beyond the mind of man, all that God has prepared for those who love him" (1 Cor 2:7–9). If God is infinite love, the happiness of our personal encounter with this loving God must infinitely surpass our own expectations.

Some New Testament images of heaven have a universal appeal for all people and ages, for example the beautiful description in chapter 21 of Revelation:

> Then I saw a new heaven and a new earth. The first heaven and the first earth disappeared, and the sea vanished. And I saw the Holy City, the new Jerusalem, coming down out of heaven from God, prepared and ready, like a bride dressed to meet her husband. I heard a loud voice speaking from the throne: "How God's home is with

mankind! He will live with them, and they shall be his people. God himself will be with them, and he will be their God. He will wipe away all tears from their eyes. There will be no more death, no more grief or crying or pain. The old things have disappeared." Then the one who sits on the throne said, "And now I make all things new!" (Rev 21:1–5).

In this description of heaven three characteristics stand out. First, newness: twice in this short text it is emphasized that everything will be made new. Second, heaven as an encounter between God and man: God will be with man, and this personal encounter will be a source of profound happiness. Third, no tears, no pain—perfect happiness: the beautiful image of God wiping away all tears like a mother symbolizes that all suffering and pain will be taken away from man. Heaven means perfect joy and happiness.

If Jesus were to describe heaven to present-day Japanese he would perhaps emphasize also other images, like music, dance, beauty, harmony, creativity, I-Thou encounter, light, humor and laughter.

Marxist Critique of Heaven:
Rival for Man's Attention to This World

Some critics of religion, for example Karl Marx, maintain that belief in a future life breeds indifference to the problems of present-day society and takes away man's energy from the task of building this earth. According to Marxist interpretation, man's belief in a future life originates from the experience of injustice on this earth; man is looking for a consolation in his misery and turns his eyes to a future heaven.

One must admit that historically some oppressed people have developed a strong sense of belief in an afterlife and have tried to project their hopes to heaven since they did not see any hope of finding happiness on this earth. The history of the blacks in America offers some examples of such projection.

However, there is no need for us to suppose such a sharp dichotomy between this life on earth and the future life in heaven. Rather, we can consider both as a unified vision. According to the Gospel of Saint John and the letters of Saint Paul, eternal life is already beginning now. Although it will bloom to its fullness only after death, it is considered to be a present reality. When eternal life is understood to be embryonically present here and now, the Marxist critique loses its sting. If one sees eternal life beginning already here on earth and sees the developing of this earth and of human history as a process that reaches into eternity, we will feel an even greater responsibility. This earth has an intrinsic worth and a great dignity both as a creation of God and as a task entrusted to man; for man is being asked to work for the full development of this earth. The Christian sees his work for a better earth as a cooperation with the eternal plan of the Creator God, consequently as a responsibility of the highest order. Not passive waiting for heaven, but, rather, active working for a better and lasting future, is the characteristic attitude of a genuine Christian.

A proper Christian interpretation of the world and of the future can give a strong motivation for creating a better world. From a psychological point of view one can ask:

Will a person be more stimulated to better this world if he believes that he himself and everything around him will be destroyed someday or if he is convinced that he himself, those he loves and his work have eternal value?

Meaning of Belief in Immortality for Man's Life Today

1. Belief in eternal life gives meaning to life now

If my whole existence is completely extinguished at the moment of death, what meaning is there in putting a lifelong effort in building up and developing this existence? If all my efforts eventually end in futility, is not life as a whole absurd? This is the most fundamental question about the meaning or absurdity of man's life. Of course, everybody will discover partial meanings in different aspects of his life. Still, one cannot be satisfied with only partial meanings. To use a comparison from language: only when the whole sentence is finished can we see whether the sentence has a meaning or not; individual words are not sufficient. Life is either totally mean ingful or totally futile, depending on whether there is any meaning in death.

When reflecting on the meaning of death we are ultimately thinking about the meaning of life. This is beautifully expressed in Cervantes' *Don Quixote*. Don Quixote tells Sancho Panza about the look he saw in the eyes of the soldiers who lay dying in his arms. He noticed that these dying eyes were asking a question. Sancho Panza asks: "Was it the question 'Why am I dying?' " Quixote replies: "No, it was the question 'Why was I living?' "

C. G. Jung has pointed out that a belief in life after death is important for the psychological health of a person:

> As a physician I am convinced that it is hygienic—if I may use the word—to discover in death a goal towards which one can strive; and that shrinking away from it is something unhealthy and abnormal

which robs the second half of life of its purpose. I therefore consider the religious teaching of a life hereafter consonant with the standpoint of psychic hygiene. . . . It happens sometimes that I must say to an older patient: Your picture of God or your idea of immortality is atrophied; consequently your metabolism is out of gear.[23]

If there is nothing at the end of life's road, then the journey of life leads nowhere. Aging man, especially, will suffer from such an illusion. For the longer the journey, the more apparent will it become that his journey has no real goal. But if even death is meaningful, if there is a true goal of man's life journey beyond the moment of death, then life with all its pains and sufferings takes on a profound meaning. Thus, man's immortality is not only a question about the eternal future of man but turns into a question about the meaning or absurdity of my life here and now.[24]

In his *Pensées*, Pascal has forcefully pointed

[23] C. G. Jung, *Modern Man in Search of a Soul* (New York: Harcourt, Brace, 1933), 112.

[24] Peter J. Kreeft, *Love Is Stronger than Death*, xvi.

to the close interrelatedness between man's immortality and a meaningful life now:

> The immortality of the soul is a matter which is of so great consequence to us, and which touches us so profoundly, that we must have lost all feeling to be indifferent as to knowing what it is. All our actions and thoughts must take such different courses, according as there are or are not eternal joys to hope for, that it is impossible to take one step with sense and judgment, unless we regulate our course by our view of this point which ought to be our ultimate end.[25]

2. Belief in eternal life can give capacity for wonder and surprise—openness to and fascination with the eternal future

Some philosophers have said that wonder is the beginning of all philosophy. Certainly, the capacity for surprise and wonder is one of the most precious abilities of man. The ability to wonder opens man's mind

[25] Blaise Pascal, *Pensées* (New York: Washington Square Press, 1965), 59.

and heart, moves him to the future and urges him to search for the unknown. The child's capacity for wonder and surprise helps him to discover the world and himself. Surprise and wonder give freshness and zest to man throughout his whole life. As a man grows older, he can, to a certain extent, preserve his youthfulness if he retains a sense of wonder and surprise; but if he loses it and cannot delight in surprise or be awed by wonder, he has become senile; in a sense, he has mentally died before his physical death.

The person who believes in life after death develops, throughout his whole life, a deep sense of wonder and surprise. For him, a great surprise is waiting after death, and this expectation and hope fills his heart, also in the later years of life, with excitement and freshness. Belief in eternal life can make the great difference in the basic attitude of man during his whole lifetime. If death extinguishes his whole existence, fear of this threatening enemy of his life is a natural reaction. For many people, the sick periods of old age become a series of boring, depressing and hopeless days filled with frustration, disillusion and bitterness. On the contrary, the person who believes in life after death can look forward, full of expectation and hope, for what tomorrow may bring. One of the best ways to master the problem of old age and to prepare for death is to develop a strong capacity for surprise and wonder.